Oregon
Real Estate Pre-License
Practice

2nd Edition

Oregon Real Estate Pre-license Practice

Executive Editor: Sara Glassmeyer

Project Manager: Arlin Kauffman,
LEAP Publishing Services

Developmental Editor: Molly Armstrong-Paschal

Art and Cover Composition: Chris Dailey

Cover Image: ProSchools

For product information and technology assistance, contact us at
OnCourse Learning and Sales Support, 1-855-733-7239.
For permission to use material from this text or product.

Library of Congress Control Number: 2015951036

ISBN-10: 1629801429
ISBN-13: 978-1-62980-142-1

OnCourse Learning
3100 Cumberland Blvd, Suite 1450
Atlanta, GA 30339
USA

Visit us at **www.oncoursepublishing.com**

Printed in the United States of America
1 2 3 4 5 6 7 20 19 18 17 16

Anti-Discrimination Laws

Overview

In this lesson we review laws against discrimination. Practices of blockbusting, steering, and redlining are explained. Penalties for violations are outlined. Finally, the Americans with Disabilities Act (ADA) is summarized with highlights of its impact on real estate activity.

Objectives

Upon completion of this lesson, the student should be able to:

1. Describe the purpose of the Civil Rights Act of 1866.
2. Describe the purpose of the Fair Housing Act of 1968.
3. Describe the purpose of the Fair Housing Amendments Act of 1988.
4. Define and give examples of blockbusting, steering and redlining.
5. Identify and describe exemptions to the fair housing laws.
6. Describe the penalties for those who violate the fair housing laws.
7. Explain the major provisions of the Americans with Disabilities Act regarding real property transactions.

Fair Housing Act

When offering real estate for sale or rent, a real estate agent must be aware of the laws pertaining to discrimination. These laws, referred to as open housing, fair housing, or equal housing opportunity laws, prohibit unfair and discriminatory practices. Their provisions affect every phase of the real estate process from listing to closing, and all real estate agents must comply with them.

In enforcing fair housing laws and regulations, government officials focus on the effect of a person's conduct rather than the person's intent. A person with the best of intentions, who means to comply with the law, will be sanctioned if his actions do not, in fact, comply with it. If the effect of one's actions or statements violates the law, good intentions may at best only mitigate the sanction that may be imposed. The potential sanctions for violation of these laws may include loss of license, civil damages and penalties and, in some cases, criminal prosecution leading to fines and/or imprisonment.

----- CIVIL RIGHTS ACT OF 1866 -----

Among the first government actions taken to eliminate discrimination in housing were the 13th Amendment to the Constitution prohibiting slavery (enacted in 1865), and the 14th Amendment to the Constitution, giving citizenship to all persons born or naturalized in the U.S. (including the freed slaves) and prohibiting states from making or enforcing laws limiting rights or denying equal protection under its laws to any persons, enacted in 1868.

To reinforce the 13th Amendment, Congress passed the **Civil Rights Act of 1866**. This law states that "all citizens of the U.S. shall have the same right, in every state and territory, as is enjoyed by white citizens thereof, to inherit, purchase, lease, sell, hold, and convey real and personal property." This law is still in effect and is still important, as it applies in some aspects to more situations than laws passed more recently.

For example, this law has no exceptions to its prohibitions with regard to race and color. While the later Civil Rights Act of 1968 prohibits discrimination on more bases than just race or color, it has a number of exceptions. Therefore, practices that might not be prohibited under the Civil Rights Act of 1968 would be prohibited under the Civil Rights Act of 1866, if they applied to racial discrimination.

For example, the Civil Rights Act of 1968 does not apply to a homeowner who:
- does not use the services of a real estate agent.
- does not advertise using discriminatory wording.
- does not sell more than one house in 24 months.
- does not own more than three homes.

However, because the Civil Rights Act of 1866 *does* apply, such a homeowner cannot discriminate on the basis of race. While the Civil Rights Act of 1968 applies only to housing, the Civil Rights Act of 1866 applies to all real and personal property transactions. Therefore, the Civil Rights Act of 1866 goes further and prohibits racial discrimination in the sale or lease of residential or commercial real property, as well as in the sale or lease of personal property and in the sale of a business.

----- CIVIL RIGHTS ACT OF 1968 -----

Title VIII of the **Civil Rights Act of 1968** prohibits discrimination in the sale, leasing and financing of housing. It has been called the **Fair Housing Act**, as its stated purpose is to provide for fair housing and equal housing opportunities throughout the United States.

Protected Classes

When originally passed, the law prohibited discrimination on the basis of race, color, religion, and national origin. The law was amended by the Housing and Community Development Act of 1974 to prohibit discrimination on the basis of sex.

The law was amended again by the **Fair Housing Amendments Act of 1988** to prohibit discrimination on the basis of familial status (persons living with, or expected to be living with, children under 18), and mental or physical handicap. Persons with a mental or physical handicap are those who have a physical or mental impairment that substantially limits any of their major life activities. Persons protected under the law would include those who have or are perceived to have:

- hearing, mobility and visual impairments.
- HIV infection (i.e., human immunodeficiency virus, including all HIV and HIV-related viruses which damage the cellular branch of the human immune system and leave the infected person immunodeficient).
- chemical sensitivity.
- chronic alcoholism.
- mental retardation.
- manic depression.

The law also protects nondisabled persons who associate or live with disabled persons.

Federal Fair Housing Act	
Prohibits discrimination on the basis of:	
<ul><li>Race</li><li>Color</li><li>Religion</li><li>Sex</li></ul>	<ul><li>Handicap</li><li>National Origin</li><li>Familial Status</li></ul>

Illegal Activities

With regard to property and transactions covered by the Fair Housing Act, certain actions based on the race, color, national origin, religion, sex, handicap or familial status of a person are illegal.

In terms of sale or rental it is illegal to:
* refuse to negotiate with a person.
* refuse to rent or sell to a person who has made a bona fide offer.
* make housing unavailable or deny housing to a person.

Thus, it would be illegal on the basis of a protected classification of a person to:
* fail to consider or accept an offer.
* impose different sales prices or rental charges.
* use different application criteria, or sale or rental standards or procedures.
* evict tenants.
* discriminate in the terms, conditions or privileges for sale or rental of housing, or in the provision of services or facilities in connection with the sale or rental of housing.
* make statements or advertisements that indicate a preference, limitation or discrimination. This applies to all written or oral notices or statements by a person engaged in the sale or rental of a dwelling. Written notices and statements include any applications, flyers, brochures, deeds, signs, banners, posters, billboards or any other documents used with respect to the sale or rental of a dwelling.
* represent that housing is not available for inspection, sale or rental when in fact it is.

In relating to persons with a handicap, it is illegal to:
* inquire to as to whether an applicant, or a person intending to reside in the dwelling after it is sold, rented or made available, has a handicap or to inquire as to the nature or severity of the handicap.
* refuse to make reasonable accommodations in rules, policies, practices, or services, if necessary for a handicapped person to use the housing.
* refuse to allow a handicapped person to make reasonable modifications to the dwelling or common use areas, at that person's expense, if:
  o they are necessary for that person to use the housing.
  o where reasonably required by the landlord, that person agrees to restore the property to its original condition when he moves.

It is illegal to engage in blockbusting. **Blockbusting** is inducing or attempting to induce, for profit, owners of housing to sell or rent by representing that persons of a certain race, color, etc., are or may be entering into the neighborhood. Blockbusting may be obvious, such as when the person creates fear of a loss in value, increase in crime, or decrease in quality of schools as a result of minorities entering a neighborhood.

	When a broker tells an owner that a Mexican-American family has purchased a house on the street where the owner's home is located in order to encourage the owner to sell his home and purchase elsewhere, this is blockbusting and a violation of the law. A real estate agent may not make representations that a change has, may, or will occur in the racial, religious, or ethnic composition of any block, neighborhood, or area in order to induce an individual to sell.
For Example	

Blockbusting may also occur unintentionally. Farming, a perfectly acceptable listing technique of becoming the "expert" in a geographical area, may lead to charges of blockbusting when practiced in areas with new or potentially new minority members.

	An agent vigorously solicits listings in an area that has a changing population without mentioning anything about the change. He may not even be aware of the changes occurring. An intensive telephone, mail, or door-to-door solicitation campaign for listings in a changing neighborhood may be just as illegal as intentional blockbusting as the effect would be the same.
For Example	

Steering is also illegal. While blockbusting relates to activity involving owners, steering relates to activity involving buyers or renters. **Steering** is restricting or attempting to restrict the choices of a person by word or conduct in connection with seeking, negotiating for, buying or renting a dwelling so as to perpetuate segregated housing patterns or to discourage or obstruct choices in a community, neighborhood or development. Steering includes channeling homeseekers to particular areas because of the presence or absence of minority neighbors. It is directing them to or from an area in order to either maintain the homogeneity of the area or change the character of an area. Showing homes to white persons only in white neighborhoods or showing homes to minorities only in minority neighborhoods would be steering. Steering would include discouraging a person from inspecting, purchasing or renting a dwelling because of his race, religion, etc. or that of persons in a community, neighborhood or development.

A lender cannot, on the basis of a protected classification of a person:
- refuse to make a residential mortgage loan.
- refuse to provide information regarding such a loan.
- impose different terms or conditions on such a loan.
- discriminate in appraising property.
- refuse to purchase a loan.
- set different terms or conditions for purchasing a loan.

It is also illegal for a lender to **redline** an area, that is, refuse to make a loan based on the racial or ethnic composition of the area.

Illegal Practices	
Blockbusting	Scaring owners into selling
Steering	Buyers taken to only certain areas
Redlining	Mortgage company stays out of certain neighborhoods

It is also illegal:

- to deny or restrict a person's access to or membership or participation in any real estate service (such as multiple listing service or real estate broker's organization) or other facilities related to the business of selling or renting housing.
- for any person whose business includes engaging in the selling, brokering or appraising of residential real property to discriminate in making services available or in performing such services.
- to threaten, coerce, intimidate, or interfere with anyone exercising a fair housing right or assisting others to exercise their fair housing right.

Exemptions

The law does not prohibit discrimination based on criteria other than race, color, national origin, religion, sex, handicap or familial status. Therefore, it is legal to discriminate on the basis of amount of income or disposable income, credit history, poor references or lack of references, past rental or employment history, length of time at current employment, smoking habits, criminal convictions, etc., unless other state or local laws prohibit such discrimination.

This law does not apply to all real property. It applies only to residential property. It does not apply to commercial, industrial or recreational property.

The law allows a religious organization to limit the sale, rental or occupancy of dwellings it owns or operates for other than commercial purposes to persons of that religion, or to give preference to such persons, as long as membership in the organization is not restricted on the basis of race, color, or national origin.

The law allows a private club to restrict occupancy of lodgings used for noncommercial purposes to its members or to give them preference.

The law provides an exemption relating to the sale or rental of a single-family home. To qualify for the exemption all of the following factors must be present:

- The home must be owned by a private individual, not a business or partnership.
- The individual cannot own more than three single-family homes at any one time.
- If the individual is not living in the dwelling, or was not the most recent occupant at the time of transaction, the exemption only applies to one sale within any 24-month period.
- If the property qualifies, the exemption will apply only if the services of a real estate agent or other person in the real estate business are not used and discriminatory advertising is not used. A person is considered in the real estate business if he:
  - is involved in three or more sales or rentals of his own properties.
  - was involved in two transactions for others within the last 12 months.
  - owns a building with more than four units.

The Fair Housing Act does not apply to the rental of rooms or units in a one- to four-family dwelling if the owner actually maintains and occupies one of the living units as his residence. It does apply to any multifamily dwelling, if the owner does not live in one of the units, and to any multifamily dwelling of five or more units even if the owner does live in one of the units.

With regard to familial status discrimination, the law exempts housing for the elderly. This is housing that:

- the Secretary of Housing and Urban Development (HUD) has determined is specifically designed for and occupied by elderly persons under a federal, state or local government program; or
- that is occupied solely by person 62 or older; or
- that houses at least one person 55 or older in at least 80% of the occupied units and adheres to policies and procedures that demonstrate an intent to house persons 55 or older.

Broker Responsibilities

To comply with this law, brokers have a number of responsibilities. A broker is required to display an equal housing opportunity poster in any place of business where housing is offered for sale or rent, including model homes. If HUD were to investigate a broker for discriminatory practices, failure to have the poster on display would be evidence of discrimination.

The broker should refuse to accept listings where the owner intends to discriminate. If an owner were to refuse an offer on a discriminatory basis, the broker should explain to the owner that such action is a violation of the law and that he is required to relate this violation to the offeror. If the owner persists, the broker should terminate the listing and request his commission.

In showing properties, the broker should refuse to provide any information regarding the minority composition of a neighborhood or base the choice of homes he shows on such composition.

In leasing property, the broker must treat families with children the same as he would treat persons without children.

In advertising, the broker must be sure he does not give the appearance of indicating preferences by referring to ethnic social clubs in the area; by using models which may by omission indicate the absence of families with children, minorities, etc.; or by using terms indicating exclusion of certain persons. The safest way to avoid discriminatory advertising is to advertise the *property* and not the people who might live there.

Enforcement

The law is administered by HUD. Any aggrieved person or HUD itself may file a complaint against a person alleged to be engaging in discriminatory housing practices; the complaint may be filed within one year after the practice occurred or terminated. The complaint must be filed in writing with HUD or a substantially equivalent state or local agency (an agency which enforces equivalent state or local laws against discrimination). In addition, the complainant may file a civil suit in state court or U. S. District Court within two years after the practice occurred or terminated, or two years after HUD had concluded its efforts to resolve the complaint.

HUD will try to have an investigation completed and reconcile the complaint within 100 days after the complaint is filed. If the investigation indicates that the complaint is valid, HUD may try to reach a conciliation agreement with the respondent, resulting in remedy of the violation and elimination or prevention of the illegal practice in the future. If the agreement is signed and later breached, HUD may recommend that the Attorney General file suit.

If an agreement cannot be reached, the case will be heard in an administrative hearing, unless either the complainant or respondent wants to be heard in U. S. District Court. In an administrative hearing, the complainant may be represented by HUD attorneys or his own attorney. If the administrative law judge holding the hearing decides discrimination occurred, he may order the respondent to:

- pay reasonable attorney fees and costs and pay compensation for actual damages (including humiliation, pain and suffering).
- pay the federal court a civil penalty of up to $16,000 for the first violation, up to $37,500 for a second violation within five years, and up to $65,000 for a third or subsequent violation within seven years.
- provide injunctive or other equitable relief, e.g., to make the housing available to the complainant.

The U.S. Attorney General may file a suit in U. S. District Court if there is reasonable cause to believe a pattern or practice of housing discrimination is occurring. He may also be authorized by HUD to go to court in cases where immediate help is necessary to stop a serious problem to seek temporary or preliminary relief pending the outcome of a complaint investigation.

----- STATE DISCRIMINATION LAWS -----

State and local governments also have laws and ordinances prohibiting the practice of discrimination in real estate transactions. These are enforced by state and local human rights departments. In Oregon it is unlawful to discriminate based on race, color, national origin, religion, gender, familial status (the presence of children in a household), disability, marital status, source of income (including, as of July 1, 2014, Housing Choice/Section 8 Vouchers), sexual orientation (including gender identity) or status as a domestic violence victim. The smaller the governmental jurisdiction, the more classes are protected. In other words, a city ordinance may protect more groups than the state statute would, and the state statute may protect more classes than the federal law would.

In addition, state license laws usually prohibit licensees from violating any local, state or federal laws prohibiting discriminatory practices. The penalty for a violation by a licensee could be license revocation.

Americans with Disabilities Act (ADA)

With the passage of the Fair Housing Amendments Act of 1988, Congress prohibited discrimination against those with physical and mental handicaps in housing. This law did not apply to any types of real property other than housing. Therefore, when Congress passed the **Americans with Disabilities Act (ADA)** in 1990 to prohibit discrimination against those with disabilities, a part of that law addressed the problem of discrimination in public accommodations and commercial facilities.

The ADA was enacted to guarantee to those with mental or physical disabilities equal opportunities to:
- employment.
- state and local government services.
- public accommodations.
- telecommunications.
- transportation.

Under the law, an individual with a disability is a person who has a physical or mental impairment that substantially limits one or more major life activities, or has a record of such an impairment, or is regarded as having such an impairment. Major life activities would include such functions as caring for oneself, performing manual tasks, walking, seeing, hearing, speaking, breathing, learning, and working. However, the law does not afford protection to individuals who currently use illegal drugs when an action is taken on the basis of that use.

Title I of the law provides that businesses with 15 or more employees may not discriminate in hiring or promotion against an individual with a disability if the person is otherwise qualified for the job. This means they must also make reasonable accommodation for such an individual in the form of restructuring the job, modifying work schedules, acquiring or modifying equipment, etc. Reasonable accommodation might include the following:
- Restructuring the job
- Modifying work schedules
- Acquiring or modifying equipment
- Modifying training materials or policies
- Providing qualified readers or interpreters to blind employees
- Modifying the existing facilities used by employees in order to make them readily accessible to and usable by an individual with a disability

The reasonableness portion of this requirement means an employer is not required to lower quality or quantity standards or impose an undue hardship on the operation of the business in order to make the accommodation. This section of the law applies to real estate firms just as it does to other business entities.

Title III of the Act addresses public accommodations and services in commercial facilities. A **public accommodation** is any private entity open to the public. It may be an owner, tenant, landlord or operator of a:

- place of lodging.
- establishment serving food or drink.
- place of exhibition or entertainment.
- place of public gathering.
- sales or retail establishment.
- service establishment.
- station used for specific public transportation.
- place of public display or collection.
- place of exercise or recreation.
- social service center establishment.

A **commercial facility** is defined as a private facility intended for nonresidential use whose operations effect commerce. This includes places of employment, such as a manufacturing facility or corporate office.

A public accommodation is prohibited from discriminating against individuals on the basis of a disability in the full and equal enjoyment of its goods, services, facilities, privileges, advantages and accommodations.

Any new construction of a commercial facility or public accommodation must be designed to be readily accessible unless it would be structurally impracticable to do so. **Readily**

 **accessible** means that disabled patrons and employees will be able to get to, enter and use the facility. Even if the structure cannot be made to offer total accessibility, it must still be structured in a manner that will enable it to comply with the requirements to the greatest extent possible.

All alterations to existing commercial facilities and public accommodations must, to the maximum extent feasible, be made in a manner readily accessible to disabled individuals. These additional accessibility alterations are only required to the extent that the added accessibility costs are not disproportionate to the overall costs of the alterations.

The law affects real estate licensees in a number of ways. Under the law, a real estate broker's office would be considered a place of public accommodation, subject to the provisions of the law requiring accessibility. In addition, the law has a considerable impact upon agents handling negotiations for the purchase or lease of commercial properties. An agent engaged in managing commercial property would be responsible for ensuring that the owner he represents is in compliance with the law.

Brain Teaser

Reinforce your understanding of the material by correctly completing the following sentences:

1. The Civil Rights Act of _____ has no exceptions to its prohibitions with regard to race and color.

2. _____ is refusing to make a loan based on the racial or ethnic composition of the area.

3. The _____ _____ _____ Act prohibits discrimination against those with disabilities in public accommodations and commercial facilities.

Brain Teaser Answers

1. The Civil Rights Act of **1866** has no exceptions to its prohibitions with regard to race and color.

2. **Redlining** is refusing to make a loan based on the racial or ethnic composition of the area.

3. The **Americans with Disabilities** Act prohibits discrimination against those with disabilities in public accommodations and commercial facilities.

Review — Anti-Discrimination Laws

In this lesson we review laws against discrimination.

Federal Discrimination Laws

The Civil Rights Act of 1866 was passed by Congress to prohibit racial discrimination in the sale or lease of residential or commercial property, as well as in the sale or lease of personal property, and in the sale of a business.

Title VIII of the Civil Rights Act of 1968 prohibits discrimination in housing. It has been called the Fair Housing Act, as its stated purpose is to provide for fair housing and equal housing opportunities throughout the U.S. It prohibits discrimination in the sale and rental of housing as well as in related services, such as residential mortgage lending. The law, as amended, prohibits discrimination on the basis of race, religion, color, sex, national origin, familial status (a family with persons under age 18), and mental or physical handicap.

Practices Prohibited by Law

Three particular practices that this law prohibits are blockbusting, steering, and redlining. Blockbusting is inducing or attempting to induce, for profit, owners of housing to sell or rent by representing that persons of a certain race, color, etc., are or may be entering into the neighborhood. Steering is restricting or attempting to restrict the choices of a person by word or conduct in connection with seeking, negotiating for, buying or renting a dwelling so as to perpetuate segregated housing patterns, or to discourage or obstruct choices in a community, neighborhood or development. Redlining occurs when a lender refuses to make or provide information regarding residential mortgage loans, imposes different terms or conditions on a loan, discriminates in appraising property, refuses to purchase a loan, or sets different terms or conditions for purchasing a loan based on the racial or ethnic composition of the area.

If asked to participate in discriminatory activity, an agent must refuse and advise the client or customer that they are in violation of the law.

Exceptions

The Fair Housing Act has exceptions. It only applies to residential property. It allows religious organizations to limit the sale, rental, or occupancy of dwellings it owns or operates (other than for commercial purposes) to persons of that religion, or to give preference to such persons, as long as membership in the organization is not restricted on the basis of race, color, or national origin. It allows private clubs that provide noncommercial lodgings to its members, to restrict occupancy to its members or to give them preference. It exempts the owner of a one- to four-family dwelling who lives in one of the units. It exempts the sale or rental of a single-family home owned by a private individual who:

- does not own more than three single-family homes at any one time.

- either lives in the home or does not sell more than one home in a 24-month period.
- is not, and does not use the services of a real estate agent.
- does not use discriminatory advertising.

The law also exempts housing for the elderly with regard to familial status discrimination.

The Fair Housing Act

The Fair Housing Act is administered by HUD. A person may file a complaint with HUD within one year, or a civil suit in state or U.S. District Court within two years, after a discriminatory practice occurred or terminated. If no agreement can be reached between the complainant and the alleged offender, the case will be heard in an administrative hearing, unless either the complainant or respondent wants to be heard in U.S. District Court. If the administrative law judge decides discrimination occurred, he may order the respondent to pay reasonable attorney fees and costs, to pay compensation for actual charges (including humiliation, pain and suffering), to pay a civil penalty of up to $16,000 for the first violation, up to $37,500 for a second violation within five years and up to $65,000 for the third violation within seven years, and to provide injunctive or other equitable relief. The U.S. Attorney General may file a suit in federal court if there is reasonable cause to believe a pattern or practice of housing discrimination is occurring.

The Americans with Disabilities Act

The Americans with Disabilities Act (ADA) was passed in order to guarantee to those with mental or physical disabilities equal opportunities to employment, state and local government services, public accommodations, telecommunications and transportation.
- **Title I** provides that employers with 15 or more employees may not discriminate against an individual with a disability in hiring or promotion if the person is otherwise qualified for the job.
- **Title III** prohibits public accommodations and services in commercial facilities from discriminating against individuals on the basis of a disability. The law requires that any new construction of a commercial facility or public accommodation be designed to be readily accessible unless it would be structurally impracticable to do so.

State Laws and License Laws

State and local laws may prohibit discrimination on the same basis as the federal law but add different categories as protected classes. In Oregon, it is also illegal to discriminate in housing transactions based on a person's marital status, source of income (including, as of July 1, 2014, Housing Choice/Section 8 Vouchers), sexual orientation (including gender identity) or status as a domestic violence victim. License laws prohibit licensees from violating the provisions of local, state or federal anti-discrimination laws.

Oregon Brokerage Relationships

Overview

This lesson explores the roles and relationships of principal brokers, brokers and licensed property managers in the real estate business. Included in the discussion are limitations on functions of unlicensed persons as well as the responsibilities of persons supervising licensed and unlicensed persons.

Objectives

Upon completion of this lesson, the student should be able to:

1. Explain the difference between independent contractors and employees.
2. Explain the duties of a licensed personal assistant.
3. Explain the duties of an unlicensed personal assistant.
4. Explain the supervisory role of the licensee employing a licensed or unlicensed personal assistant.
5. Explain the license requirement for having a licensed personal assistant.
6. Explain the requirements for a real estate office and its signage.
7. Explain the role of the principal broker regarding supervision of affiliated licensees.
8. Describe the required procedures when a licensee leaves a brokerage firm voluntarily or the principal broker terminates the licensee.

Real Estate Professionals

----- REAL ESTATE BROKERAGE -----

A real estate **brokerage firm** performs professional real estate activity. To do so legally, it must meet criteria established by the state for setting up any other type of business and register with the Oregon Real Estate Agency.

All real estate activity performed by a principal broker or a broker associated with a principal broker is performed on behalf of the real estate brokerage. The real estate company has the listings. It enters contracts with the multiple listing service, the advertisers and office suppliers. It has full control over its staff and is responsible for their actions.

The brokerage company need not be owned by anyone eligible to perform professional real estate activity. An unlicensed person could own a real estate brokerage, but he would have to contract with a person who is licensed as a principal broker to be responsible for the supervision of all real estate activity in the company.

To start a real estate brokerage, a principal broker will register a company business name. If he does not own the business, he must obtain the permission of the owner to use the business name.

Within the company, any number of persons may be licensed to perform professional real estate activity. In addition to the principal broker who registers the company, the company may have:
- other principal brokers, equally qualified by experience, education and examination to have supervisory roles within the company.
- brokers who are eligible to perform all types of professional real estate activity but are not eligible to supervise any licensees.
- licensed property managers, eligible to perform only those activities relating to management of rental property.
- unlicensed employees, who may:
  - perform technical and clerical functions and who may perform activities as personal assistants for brokers.
  - be engaged in activities related to renting and leasing real estate, except soliciting new property management business, on behalf of the principal broker.

The license law designates licensees associated with a principal broker as agents of the principal broker. Whether licensed as a broker or as a property manager, a licensee associated with a principal broker performs real estate activity on behalf of the principal broker. This makes that licensee an agent of the principal broker and, under agency law, makes the principal broker liable for acts of those licensees performed within the scope of the agency.

----- INDEPENDENT CONTRACTORS -----

 Nothing in the law prevents the establishment of an independent contractor relationship between real estate licensees or requires the establishment of an employer-employee relationship. A principal broker may choose to classify an associated licensee as an employee or as an independent contractor. While there are advantages and disadvantages to both the employee relationship and the independent contractor relationship in a real estate company, the most prevalent relationship in Oregon, as well as the rest of the nation, is that of independent contractor.

As an employee, an individual is subject to the complete control of his employer, both on the result and the means used to obtain the result.

As an independent contractor, an individual is retained to perform certain tasks. The party retaining him may require a certain result, such as the sale of real estate, but may not control the means used to reach that result.

Under Oregon income tax law (ORS 316.209) and workers' compensation law (ORS 656.037), a real estate licensee may be considered an independent contractor if he meets all of the following criteria of a **qualified real estate agent**:
- He is a real estate licensee under ORS 696.010 to 696.490.
- Substantially all of the remuneration (whether or not paid in cash) for his services as a real estate licensee is directly related to sales or other output (including the performance of services) rather than to the number of hours worked.
- His services are performed under the terms of a written contract between him and his principal broker, and the contract provides that he will not be treated as an employee with respect to the services for Oregon tax purposes.

Under federal tax laws, a number of practical tests are applied to determine an acceptable independent contractor relationship. Failure to meet any of these tests could invalidate an independent contractor relationship and cause additional tax or other liabilities for both parties. As a result of these tests, a principal broker usually does not:
- withhold federal and state income taxes from the affiliated broker's earnings;
- pay federal Social Security (FICA) or state workers' compensation costs of the independent contractor;
- include the independent contractor in any company-sponsored retirement or pension plan;
- pay license fees or professional membership fees for the independent contractor;
- reimburse the independent contractor for business expenses (e.g., car, travel, meals, lodging); and
- pay a minimum salary to the independent contractor.

The principal broker may, however, require minimum floor time, attendance at training sessions and completion of required continuing education courses.

As an independent contractor, a licensee may work with limited supervision by his principal broker and may not be subject to company-required sales quotas. He may enjoy income tax advantages from the deduction of business expenses not reimbursed by his principal broker, and he may also set up his own retirement program.

----- Nonlicensed Persons -----

Many people work in real estate offices without a real estate license, assuming day-to-day duties related to various aspects of the licensed activities. An unlicensed property manager may perform many functions through the employing principal broker. An unlicensed employee (e.g., a receptionist or administrative assistant) of the principal broker or an unlicensed personal assistant of a broker may carry out numerous clerical and secretarial functions and support tasks so that licensees have more time to devote to professional real estate activity. He can:

- answer the telephone, take messages, and forward calls.
- follow up on completion of contingency requirements in transactions, including arranging for repairs and checking the progress of required financing.
- schedule appointments for licensees to show listings.
- prepare advertising copy for review, approval, and use by the principal broker.
- install signs and lockboxes on listed property.
- type and mail documents involved in transactions.
- verify the accuracy of listing information supplied by brokers, by checking the records at the county tax assessor's office.
- transmit information included in prior advertisements to a phone prospect (but not transmit information from the MLS or any other source to the prospect, even if no one else is in the office, since that would be considered sales activity).

An unlicensed employee could not legally:

- engage in cold calling, soliciting persons to buy or sell real estate.
- engage in real estate marketing.
- engage in negotiations with clients and customers in a transaction.
- answer questions on listings from information other than that included in prior advertisements.
- show real estate to prospective purchasers.
- hold open houses. While only a licensee can hold or conduct an open house, an unlicensed assistant could be present to distribute promotional materials that had been approved by the supervising broker. However, the unlicensed assistant could not engage in any professional real estate activity (e.g., activity that would result in bringing together a ready, willing and able buyer with a seller in an effort to complete a sale).

A principal broker hired a number of hostesses at $100 per day to show property. They pass out brochures, quote prices and state the terms of sale of the real property. They do not sign any agreements or other documents, as there is a real estate broker at the property to negotiate with the buyers and fill out all of the purchase and sale agreements and other pertinent documents. Under these circumstances, the hostesses and the principal broker who hired them are still in violation of the license law. To perform the activities they are performing, the hostesses would have to have real estate licenses. Even though they do not fill out or sign documents, they cannot show the houses or quote prices or terms; that is all considered part of solicitation and negotiation. All they can do is greet people, distribute promotional material and perhaps take down names of visitors. Once they go beyond that, they are soliciting and negotiating and in need of a license. The fact that the hostesses were on a per diem basis or a salary basis is irrelevant, since the law prohibits payment or receipt of compensation in any form for such unlicensed activity.

An unlicensed person could not be paid a share of an employing licensee's commission, or be paid contingent on the closing of sales by the employing licensee. An unlicensed person may be compensated on an hourly basis, a salary basis, or a flat-fee basis, but not on a commission basis.

----- PLACE OF BUSINESS -----

A principal broker not associated with another principal broker must maintain in Oregon a **place of business** specified in his license application and designated as his main office in his license. If he does not have an office, he may apply for an inactive license, which is maintained at the Agency until it is activated. If he later applies to have the license activated, it will be sent to and maintained at his principal place of business.

The office must be in Oregon, unless the principal broker is licensed in another state and holds an Oregon reciprocal license. It must have an identification sign, and have facilities  to maintain required real estate records. A person from another state can hold either a regular Oregon license or a reciprocal license. With a regular license he must have a place of business Oregon. With a reciprocal license he must have a place of business in his home state, and he cannot have a place of business in Oregon. He can come into the state to engage in transactions, but he cannot work out of an office here.

A licensee may conduct and supervise the business of more than one office, whether a main office or a branch office. A principal broker may establish any number of branch offices as separate business locations under his management, provided each branch office location is registered by providing the Commissioner with a form showing the street and mailing addresses of the branch office location and a fee.

A branch office is defined as any business location other than the main office, where professional real estate activity is regularly conducted or which is advertised to the public as a place where such business may be regularly conducted. However, a **model unit** is not considered a branch office as long as it is a permanent residential structure located in a subdivision or development, is used for distribution and dissemination of information, rather than as a place to transact sales activity, and is at all times available for sale, lease, lease option or exchange.

Also, a **temporary structure** used solely for the dissemination of information and distribution of lawfully required public reports is not considered a branch office. However, if a principal broker wanted to place a booth, regularly staffed by licensees, in a local shopping mall to display information on listings, he would need to register the booth as a branch office, since it is not a temporary structure used only to pass out information.

A principal broker's office must have a **business sign** containing the name under which he is licensed. He may not display any other business name at the place of business named in his license. The sign requirement does not authorize him to maintain an office or an office sign in conflict with any local zoning regulations, local ordinances or state laws. When he ceases to engage in professional real estate activity at and vacates any business location, he must see that his name or the name under which he has operated is removed from that location. Before changing a business location, the principal broker must notify the Commissioner in writing of the new location. If he ceases to maintain a place of business designated as a main office, he must relinquish his real estate license to the state and release the licenses of all brokers associated with him through the eLicense system of the Real Estate Agency to the Commissioner.

Supervision

A principal broker must supervise and control all professional real estate activity in his firm conducted under his name or the registered business name. He must exercise supervision over the activities of licensees associated with him, whether they are principal brokers, real estate brokers, property managers or nonlicensed employees.

This requirement for supervision does not require that he establish an employer-employee relationship or prevent him from establishing an independent contractor relationship with other licensees. He is responsible for reasonable supervision of his licensees and their real estate activities, regardless of whether the licensees are called independent contractors or employees.

The Administrative Rules of the Real Estate Agency (OAR 863-15-0140) talks about a real estate principal broker's **supervision** responsibilities. First of all, the rule says that a principal broker may not just allow a broker to use the principal broker's license for the purpose of allowing brokers to engage in professional real estate activity without the principal broker's supervision. A principal broker must supervise and control the professional real estate activity at any main or branch office registered by the principal broker. In particular, the rules say the principal broker must review each document of agreement generated in a real estate transaction within seven banking days after it has been accepted, rejected or withdrawn. If the transaction is in a branch office, the principal broker branch manager may review the documents of that branch. The document review may be done electronically or by hard copy. In either case, the principal broker should make a record of the review.

Whether the relationship of the associates to the principal broker is that of an independent contractor or an employee, the principal broker should enter into a written employment or independent contractor agreement with each associate licensee. The agreement is a personal contract for services to be performed by individuals licensed to the principal broker. It should specify:
- the broker's status as an independent contractor or employee.
- compensation arrangements, including the manner in which the broker will be paid.
- the actual duties to be performed in the office and in the field by the broker on behalf of the principal broker.
- any restrictions and requirements of performance consistent with the broker's status.

It may require that the broker will follow current and amended office procedures, but will not specify those office procedures.

Company Policy
In addition to the employment or independent contractor agreement, the principal broker should provide the associates with written policies and procedures:
- regarding the types of relationships real estate licensees associated with the company may establish.
- regarding the supervision and control of affiliated licensees in the fulfillment of their duties and obligations to their respective clients;

- regarding the supervision of licensed personal assistants employed by the brokerage or employed by licensees associated with the brokerage.
- on how licensees associated with the business will comply with the various agency relationships allowed under Oregon law.
- to ensure the protection of confidential information.
- setting forth the degree of direct principal broker supervision over affiliated principal brokers. However, the principal broker must still review each document or agreement generated by any affiliated licensee in a transaction within seven banking days after it has been accepted, rejected or withdrawn. If the document or agreement originates in a branch office, it may be reviewed by the broker who is the manager of the branch office. At the time of review, the principal broker or branch office manager must initial and date the document in writing.
- setting forth all other company procedures and performance standards in reasonable detail. Merely having a procedures manual and referencing it in the licensee agreement will not ensure licensees will comply, so the principal broker needs to supervise and enforce the procedures listed in the manual in order for it to be effective.

Personal Assistants

Personal assistants may be licensed brokers who are authorized to perform the same functions as any other licensed broker, or they may be unlicensed. Most personal assistants are unlicensed.

Whether licensed or unlicensed, a personal assistant is subject to the control and supervision of the employing licensee and that licensee's principal broker in his day-to-day activities. The employing licensee and the licensee's principal broker are responsible for the supervision and control of the personal assistant's real estate-related activities. They are both responsible for preventing unlicensed professional real estate activity by the personal assistant, and both may be liable if the unlicensed personal assistant does engage in unlicensed professional real estate activity.

A personal assistant with a broker license may help his employing broker in all phases of professional real estate activity, may share in the real estate commissions and even be paid only from commissions coming from successful closings. A licensed personal assistant must be licensed with the principal broker of the company in which he is working as a personal assistant. He may not be licensed with one principal broker and perform personal assistant functions for a principal broker in another company, or for a broker licensed with another principal broker.

A broker may directly compensate a licensed personal assistant under the terms of a licensed personal assistant agreement if he obtains a principal broker license. Generally, written office policies and the terms of a licensed personal assistant agreement will

specify responsibility for supervision and control compensation of the licensed personal assistant. The agreement should include the following:

- The name of the real estate business
- The parties to the agreement
- The duration of the agreement and a provision for its termination
- The employment status of the licensed personal assistant
- The name of the principal broker(s) with whom the licensed personal assistant is associated and reference to the written office policies and agreements establishing supervision and control of the licensed personal assistant
- The duties and responsibilities of the licensed personal assistant, including any limitations on their ability to represent clients on behalf of the broker
- The manner and means by which the licensed personal assistant is to be compensated, including reference to any principal broker authorization necessary

Multiple Principal Brokers

Once licensed as a principal broker, a licensee is able to supervise other licensees.

A real estate business may have two or more principal real estate brokers operating under the same registered business name. If two or more principal brokers are in business together, they may have equal supervisory control over and will be equally responsible for the conduct of other principal brokers or brokers associated with them, or other nonlicensed persons employed by them.

The principal broker is required to enter into written agreements with other principal brokers under which he supervises the other principal brokers, who, in turn, have authority to supervise other brokers and unlicensed persons. In these agreements, the principal brokers would establish office policies specifying the supervisory control and responsibility for each principal broker who is a party to the agreement.

For example, a principal broker may have principal brokers associated with him manage the day-to-day activities of branch offices. However, this does not relieve the principal broker of the responsibility to make sure that other principal brokers are performing adequately; he remains responsible for all branch office management decisions.

Supervision and Ownership

The responsibility for the conduct of licensees and employees is never based on the ownership of the brokerage. Therefore, while the law requires that the principal broker be active in control and supervision of the real estate activity conducted under his license, it allows a nonlicensed person or an affiliated broker to own a real estate brokerage, provided he does not attempt to control the brokerage's real estate activities.

There is no requirement that the owner of the brokerage have a real estate license. A nonlicensed person may have an ownership interest in any business through which a real estate broker or principal real estate broker engages in professional real estate activity. He may be an officer of the company, but he may not control or supervise the professional real estate activity of any real estate broker or of a principal real estate broker licensed to control or supervise the professional real estate activity of the business.

For Example	Robert Mosher owns Mosher Mart, Inc., which conducts professional real estate activity in Oregon. Mosher is not required to hold any real estate license. Responsibility for the real estate activities of the brokerage falls on the principal broker hired by Mosher, not on Mosher.

A real estate broker who is employed, engaged or supervised by a principal real estate broker could have an ownership interest in any business through which the principal broker conducts professional real estate activity. However, the broker may not employ, engage or otherwise supervise the professional activities of another broker or principal broker. He may not control or supervise the principal broker's professional real estate activity and may not interfere with or be responsible for the training and supervision of any other broker.

For Example	Harry Lee is a broker licensed with Blue Lake Brokerage, Inc., a "100% shop." This means he gets the whole commission from each sale he makes, but he pays a monthly fee to the firm for the use of its facilities. Janet Young, another licensed broker, owns the firm. Robert Neal is the principal broker. Under the law, Neal must control the real estate activities of both Lee and Young.

If a principal real estate broker operates two or more affiliated or subsidiary entities registered at the same time, the principal broker may operate separately through each such affiliated or subsidiary entity. However, the principal broker must control and supervise the professional real estate activity conducted through each affiliated and subsidiary entity.

Affiliated organizations are organizations whose controlling ownership interests (i.e., 51% or more) are owned by the same licensee(s) or entity(ies). A subsidiary business organization is one in which the majority of the voting stock or controlling ownership interest is owned by another organization.

As a general rule only a principal real estate broker can control or supervise the professional real estate activities of another real estate broker. A principal broker cannot permit the use of his license to enable other real estate licensees to engage in any professional real estate activity where his only interest is the receipt of a fee for use of his license by others, or where he has little to no supervision of the professional real estate activity conducted under his license. He cannot state or imply to current or prospective licensees or to the public that the licensees associated with him are not fully subject to his supervision or are not acting as his agents.

Extended Absence

A principal broker who intends to be absent from the company for an extended period of time may delegate his supervisory duties by authorizing another principal broker or a broker who has three years of active experience as a real estate broker to control and supervise the professional real estate activity conducted by or through the authorizing principal broker in his absence. The licensee put in charge in a principal broker's absence does not have to be licensed with the same company.

In order to be effective, the authorization must be written and signed by the authorizing licensee and the licensee accepting supervisory responsibility. It will specify a period of the licensee's absence, not to exceed 90 days. Both the authorizing licensee and the licensee authorized to act in the absence of the authorizing licensee will have joint responsibility for all professional real estate activity conducted during the authorizing licensee's absence.

A signed copy of the authorization must be filed with the Commissioner prior to the effective date of the authorization. Fax transmission of the temporary authorization is not acceptable. The document must have original signatures of the licensees involved. The Commissioner may allow a later filing if good cause can be shown, for example, the authorizing broker was called away on an emergency.

Liability

A violation of the law or an Agency rule by one licensee is not necessarily cause for the suspension or revocation of the license of another licensee engaged by or associated with the violating licensee. However, if the Commissioner determines that the principal broker had knowledge of the act constituting a violation, his license could be subject to a suspension or revocation as well. This determination by the Commissioner would arise from evidence showing that the principal broker had knowledge of a consistent and persistent pattern of improper behavior by the licensee, in which case the principal broker would be held liable.

Terminating the Relationship

The relationship between a principal broker and an associate licensee may be severed quite easily by the principal broker or the associated licensee. When it is, the license of the associate licensee is removed by the eLicense system from the principal broker's supervision.

By use of the eLicense system of the Real Estate Agency, a licensee may:

- transfer his license, to become associated with, a new principal broker, after providing written notice, personally or by certified mail, to his current principal broker.
- obtain authorization to use a registered business name to conduct professional real estate activity, after providing written notice of the change to the authorized licensee for the current registered business name.

The Real Estate Agency will transfer the license of an active associated broker or principal broker, or of a licensee who has been inactive for no more than 30 days, to a receiving principal broker with the use of the eLicense system.

A principal broker remains responsible for a licensee until the Agency receives notice through the eLicense system that the associated licensee has inactivated his license, or by the principal broker transferring the licensee out of his company using eLicense.

The license law does not govern the principal broker's payment of any compensation owed an associate licensee. Therefore, the relationship between the principal broker and the associated licensee may be severed regardless of whether all commissions due the associated licensee have been paid, and regardless of whether there is even any agreement that commissions may be due and will be paid.

The suspension or revocation of a principal broker's license will automatically suspend every license of any licensee engaged by the principal broker pending a transfer of the license. A licensee may request transfer within 30 days after the effective date of the suspension or revocation of the principal broker's license, upon payment of a transfer fee. After 30 days, the license could be transferred only upon payment of a reactivation fee.

Death and Incapacity

The relationship between a principal broker and associate licensees may also be severed if the principal broker dies or becomes incapacitated and there is no other principal broker in the company to continue the real estate activities. The law allows the associate licensees to transfer to another company and provides for appointment of a temporary licensee to oversee the orderly conclusion of the affairs of existing clients.

Upon a written request, the Commissioner may issue a **temporary license** to the executor, administrator or personal representative of the estate of a deceased broker, to the court-appointed fiduciary of an incapacitated broker, or to some other person designated by the

Commissioner, to continue to transact the business on behalf of an incapacitated broker or to wind up the affairs of a deceased or incapacitated broker. The holder of the temporary license need not have the education or other qualifications of a real estate broker, but he is subject to the same laws and rules as the holder of a broker license while engaging in professional real estate activity under the terms of the temporary license.

The term of a temporary license cannot exceed one year from the date of issuance, unless the Commissioner agrees to extend the term, based upon sufficient cause being furnished to the Commissioner by the temporary licensee.

In winding up the affairs of a deceased broker, the temporary licensee may not:
- continue to seek offers on outstanding listings after the broker's death.
- enter into any new listing or sale agreements.
- in any way conduct professional real estate activity for others who are not principals in a current contract.

At the time of the broker's death, the temporary licensee is responsible for the following:
- He must close or terminate transactions that are in various stages of completion or termination
- He must terminate all listings and buyer's service agreements on which there are no outstanding offers or signed earnest money receipts
- He must terminate all property management agreements which are in force
- He must notify immediately each listing property owner of the broker's death, the cancellation of their listing agreement and the options available to them in obtaining the services of a new broker to handle the marketing and sale of their property
- He must immediately discontinue advertising the deceased broker's listings, cancel outstanding orders for advertising properties and discontinue advertising rental property managed by the deceased broker

A temporary licensee would be entitled to perform the following activities:
- Complete negotiations between buyers and sellers on open transactions
- Deposit and withdraw money from the broker's clients' trust account in connection with the completion of all transactions pending at the time of the broker's death
- Disburse earnest money or other funds according to any outstanding earnest money receipt or other agreement
- Promptly pay all real estate commissions owing after closing of all transactions, both to the deceased broker's estate and to participating brokers entitled to commissions resulting from the transactions

The temporary licensee is responsible for collecting and disbursing all commissions due, and settling all commission disputes. The responsibility to pay out the commissions applies to payment of commissions earned on transactions closed before or after the broker's death. If a commission due to a former licensee from a transaction closed in escrow is disbursed during the time the temporary licensee is conducting the business, the temporary licensee must be paid the commission and then disburse it directly to the former licensee rather than to his new principal broker. If a transaction involves payment of a deferred commission to the licensee, arrangements need to be made for payment of the commission due after the deceased broker's brokerage is closed.

After closing the deceased broker's business, the temporary licensee must notify the Agency of the closure and of the storage location for the closed records of the brokerage.

Upon the death of a principal broker, all licenses issued under that principal broker must be immediately released to the Agency. The temporary licensee should make reasonable attempts to notify the licensees of the return of their licenses to the Agency.

----- INACTIVE LICENSES -----

A license is placed on **inactive** status once the Commissioner receives notice through the eLicense system from either the licensee terminating the relationship with the principal broker, or the principal broker terminating the licensee.

During the following 30 calendar days, the licensee may through the use of eLicense:
- Reactivate the licensee with the same principal broker
- Pay a transfer fee to change their license status and transfer to a new principal broker.
- If qualified, change the license category and status to become licensed as a principal broker, or if never before licensed as a principal broker, submit an application and pay the applicable license fee.

After the 30 days, the license may only be reactivated by applying for reactivation and paying a reactivation fee.
While the license is on inactive status, the licensee may not engage in or advertise or hold himself out as engaging in professional real estate activity in Oregon. However, after his license has become inactive, he may still be disciplined by the commissioner for actions which would have been sanctioned under an active license. If not suspended or revoked, and inactive license may be left inactive and later renewed as an inactive license or it may be reactivated.

An inactive license may be renewed every two years with payment of a $110 renewal fee. It may be reactivated upon application for reactivation, payment of the $75 reactivation fee, and completion of any required continuing education. To reactivate a license that has been renewed as an inactive license, the licensee, during the 24 months prior to the issuance of the active license, must complete the 30 hours of continuing education required for renewal of an active license.

If a license is activated within 60 days after an inactive renewal, it will be treated as an active renewal, so the cost will total $230 for the renewal/reactivation.

After his license has been inactive for two consecutive years, to reactivate the license, the inactive licensee must not only show compliance with the continuing education requirements, but must also pass a reactivation examination.

----- LICENSE SURRENDER -----

A real estate licensee may at any time submit a form to the Commissioner to surrender his license. Upon surrender, all rights under the surrendered license are terminated, except that the Commissioner retains jurisdiction to investigate the professional real estate activity conducted under the license and to take disciplinary action against the licensee under the license law.

A surrendered license cannot be renewed. After surrendering his existing license, a licensee can reenter the business by applying for a license as a new applicant.

Brain Teaser

Reinforce your understanding of the material by correctly completing the following sentences:

1. The _____ broker will be responsible for the professional real estate activity conducted on behalf of the company.

2. An unlicensed person could not be paid a share of an employing licensee's _____.

3. The Agency may determine whether supervision is adequate, based on the principal broker's written agreements and office policies and the reasonableness of his _____ taken to carry out the agreements and policies.

4. The term of a temporary license cannot exceed ___ year(s) from the date of issuance.

Brain Teaser Answers

1. The **principal** broker will be responsible for the professional real estate activity conducted on behalf of the company.

2. An unlicensed person could not be paid a share of an employing licensee's **commission**.

3. The Agency may determine whether supervision is adequate, based on the principal broker's written agreements and office policies and the reasonableness of his **actions** taken to carry out the agreements and policies.

4. The term of a temporary license cannot exceed **one** year from the date of issuance.

Review — Oregon Brokerage Relationships

This lesson explores the roles and relationship of principal brokers, brokers and licensed property managers in the real estate business.

Real Estate Brokerage

All real estate activity performed by a principal broker or a broker associated with a principal broker is performed on behalf of the real estate brokerage. An unlicensed person could own a real estate brokerage, but he would have to hire a person who is licensed as a principal broker to be responsible for the supervision of all real estate activity in the company. To start a real estate brokerage, a principal broker or sole principal broker will register a company business name. Licensees associated with a principal broker are agents of the principal broker.

A principal broker may choose to classify an associated licensee as an employee or as an independent contractor. As an employee, an individual is subject to the complete control of his employer, both on the result and the means used to obtain the result. As an independent contractor, an individual may be required to produce a certain result, such as the sale of real estate, but may not be controlled as to the means used to reach that result. A real estate licensee may be considered an independent contractor if he is a real estate licensee; substantially all of his remuneration is directly related to sales or other output, rather than to the number of hours worked; and his services are performed under the terms of a written contract that provides that he will not be treated as an employee for Oregon tax purposes.

Nonlicensed persons may carry out numerous clerical and secretarial functions and support tasks. They cannot, however, be paid a share of an employing licensee's commission or be paid contingent on the closing of sales by the employing licensee.

A sole principal broker or principal broker must maintain in Oregon a place of business open to the public, with an identification sign, and with facilities to maintain required real estate records.

A sole principal broker or principal broker may establish any number of branch offices as separate business locations under his management, provided each branch office location is registered. A model unit or a temporary structure used solely for the dissemination of information is not considered a branch office. A broker's office must have a business sign containing the name under which he is licensed.

Supervision

A sole principal broker or principal broker must supervise and control all professional real estate activity in his firm. The Agency may determine whether supervision is adequate, based on the principal broker's written agreements and office policies and the reasonableness of his actions taken to carry out the agreements and policies.

Whether the relationship of an associate to the principal broker is that of an independent contractor or an employee, the principal broker should enter into a written employment or independent contractor agreement with each associate licensee, specifying the broker's status as an independent contractor or employee, compensation arrangements, and any restrictions and requirements of performance.

A principal broker must directly supervise the licensees associated with the brokerage in the fulfillment of their duties and obligations to their respective clients under a written company policy that sets forth the types of relationships real estate licensees associated with the company may establish.

A personal assistant is subject to the control and supervision of the employing licensee and that licensee's principal broker in his day-to-day activities.

A nonlicensed person or an affiliated broker may own a real estate brokerage, provided he does not attempt to control the brokerage's real estate activities.

A sole principal broker or principal broker who intends to be absent from the company for an extended period of time may authorize another broker, sole principal broker or principal broker to control and supervise professional real estate activity during his absence for up to 90 days, in writing. The authorization must be signed by both the authorizing licensee and the licensee accepting supervisory responsibility and filed with the Commissioner prior to the effective date of the authorization.

A violation of any of the provisions of the license law or any Agency rule by a licensee is cause for suspension or revocation of the license of a licensee associated with or engaged by him, if the Commissioner determines that the associated or engaged licensee had guilty knowledge of the act.

The principal broker may at any time release the license of an associate licensee under his supervision to the Agency. In addition, if a licensee associated with him requests that he terminate their business relationship, he must, without delay release the license to the Commissioner.

In the event of the death or incapacity of a principal broker or sole principal broker of a real estate business, the Commissioner may issue a temporary license to a person to continue to transact the business or wind up the affairs of the deceased broker. The temporary license is effective for up to one year.

After a license has been released to the Commissioner, it is placed on inactive status.

Oregon Compensation

Overview

This lesson explores issues relating to payment of compensation to licensed and unlicensed persons in a real estate transaction.

Objectives

Upon completion of this lesson, the student should be able to:

1. Explain with whom commissions can and cannot be shared.
2. Explain how commissions are shared.
3. Explain how commissions can legally be reduced to save a sales transaction.
4. Explain when out-of-state-licensees can share commissions.

Commission

Oregon statute prohibits the sharing of real estate commissions with unlicensed persons to protect consumers by assuring they will be served only by licensed professionals. In any efforts to solicit business, a licensee must remember that Oregon's law prohibits the sharing of commissions with a person who is not licensed in this state or in another state or country.

 ORS 696.290

Sharing compensation with or paying finder's fee to unlicensed person prohibited; exceptions. (1)(a) Except as provided in paragraph (b) of this subsection, a real estate licensee may not offer, promise, allow, give, pay or rebate, directly or indirectly, any part or share of the licensee's compensation arising or accruing from any real estate transaction or pay a finder's fee to any person who is not a real estate licensee licensed under ORS 696.022.

(b) A real estate broker or principal real estate broker may pay a finder's fee or a share of the licensee's compensation on a cooperative sale when the payment is made to a licensed real estate broker in another state or country, provided that:

(A) The state or country in which the nonresident real estate broker is licensed has a law permitting real estate brokers to cooperate with real estate brokers or principal real estate brokers in this state; and

(B) The nonresident real estate broker does not conduct in this state any acts constituting professional real estate activity and for which compensation is paid. If a country does not license real estate brokers, the payee must be a citizen or resident of the country and represent that the payee is in the business of real estate brokerage in the other country.

(2) A real estate broker associated with a principal real estate broker may not accept compensation from any person other than the principal real estate broker with whom the real estate broker is associated at the time.

(3) A principal real estate broker may not make payment to the real estate broker of another principal real estate broker except through the principal real estate broker with whom the real estate broker is associated.

(4) Nothing in this section prevents payment of compensation earned by a real estate broker or principal real estate broker while licensed because of the real estate broker's or principal real estate broker's association with a different principal real estate broker or because of inactivation of the real estate broker's or principal real estate broker's license.

(5) Nothing in subsection (1) of this section prohibits a real estate licensee who has a property management agreement with the owner of a residential building or facility from authorizing the payment of a referral fee, rent credit or other compensation to an existing tenant of the owner or licensee, or a former tenant if the former tenant resided in the building or facility within the previous six months, as compensation for referring new tenants to the licensee.

(6)(a) Nothing in subsection (1) of this section prevents an Oregon real estate broker or principal real estate broker from sharing compensation on a cooperative nonresidential real estate transaction with a person who holds an active real estate license in another state or country, provided:

(A) Before the out-of-state real estate licensee performs any act in this state that constitutes professional real estate activity, the licensee and the cooperating Oregon real estate broker or principal real estate broker agree in writing that the acts constituting professional real estate activity conducted in this state will be under the supervision and control of the cooperating Oregon broker and will comply with all applicable Oregon laws;

(B) The cooperating Oregon real estate broker or principal real estate broker accompanies the out-of-state real estate licensee and the client during any property showings or negotiations conducted in this state; and

(C) All property showings and negotiations regarding nonresidential real estate located in this state are conducted under the supervision and control of the cooperating Oregon real estate broker or principal real estate broker.

(b) As used in this subsection, "nonresidential real estate" means real property that is improved or available for improvement by commercial structures or five or more residential dwelling units.

The fact that a real estate licensee cannot "offer, promise, allow, give, pay or rebate, directly or indirectly, any part or share of his commission or compensation arising or accruing from any real estate transaction or pay a finder's fee to any person who is not a real estate licensee" licensed under the license law makes it very difficult for a licensee to share his commission with an unlicensed person if that person performed any service for which a license was required, or to even pay finders' and referral fees to an unlicensed person who has nothing to do with the transaction itself.

A **finder's fee** is compensation for finding, referring or recommending a prospective client or customer interested in professional real estate activity. A broker may not share his commission with, or pay, any fee to the seller's attorney or to an investment counselor, or to a neighbor or to a friend who refers a buyer to him.

<table>
<tr><td>For Example</td><td>J.A. King, a broker in Willamette, Oregon, got a phone call from Susan Sharp, a friend in Chicago. Mrs. Sharp explained that her business partner, Tom Gordon, would be moving to Willamette in a month and would be looking for a three-bedroom home. The Gordons later bought a home through Broker King, and King paid Mrs. Sharp $75 for the referral. Broker King acted contrary to license law, even though the amount involved was only $75.</td></tr>
</table>

A person receiving a share of a commission or compensation, or even a referral fee, must hold a license that would entitle him to receive compensation for the transaction. Therefore, a broker may pay a finder's fee to a licensed property manager only if the referral relates to property management, rental or leasing. This is because a property manager license authorizes the property manager to engage only in property management activity for others for compensation. Since such property management activity would include only management, rental and leasing activity, the property manager cannot be compensated for any activity relating to the sale, lease-option or exchange of real property. Since he cannot be compensated for performing that activity, he cannot share a commission with someone who does. Neither can he receive a referral fee or finder's fee relating to that activity. It would be illegal for a licensee to pay the property manager and illegal for the property manager to accept payment.

On the other hand, a licensed property manager could pay a referral fee, a finder's fee, or a commission to a principal broker, broker (through the principal broker) or other property manager for finding a prospective renter for one of the property manager's rental properties, or for referral of owners for property management services. This is because the broker, principal broker and property manager are authorized, by virtue of their licenses, to engage in property management activity for a fee, even if they have decided not to engage in such activities.

----- SHARING COMMISSIONS -----

A principal broker may share commissions directly with other property managers or principal brokers, but he may not make payment to the broker of another principal broker except through the principal broker with whom the broker is associated. A broker associated with a principal broker may not accept compensation from any person other than the principal broker with whom he is associated at the time he earned the compensation.

For Example	A broker associated with Broker A cannot be paid any compensation from Broker B or from Property Manager C, and Broker B or Property Manager C cannot pay the broker associate except through Broker A.

A principal broker receives the commission as provided for in the agreement with his client and, in turn, pays the affiliated broker in accordance with the commission split schedule to

 which they have agreed in writing. The right to payment of earned commissions is not lost by transferring a license to another principal broker prior to payment of the commission by the client. Nothing in the statute is intended to prevent payment of a commission or fee earned by a broker or principal broker while licensed due to his change of affiliation or inactivation of his license.

If the license is transferred prior to payment of an earned commission arising from a closing or deferred commission, the principal broker with whom the licensee was associated at the time the commission was earned may, and has an obligation to, directly pay the licensee the portion of the commission earned. Therefore, a principal broker may pay a commission or fee to a licensee who is currently associated with him or who had been associated with him at the time the commission or fee was earned, even if that person is subsequently associated with another broker or has an inactive license or an expired license at the time of payment.

When a licensee lists or produces a buyer for a property while associated with Broker A, that licensee would be entitled to compensation for the activity from Broker A even if he is no longer licensed with Broker A, or with anybody, at the time the commission is paid. In this case, Broker A, the former principal broker, is not splitting a commission with Broker B, the licensee's current firm, but rather simply paying that portion or a part of that portion of the commission to which the licensee would have been entitled had he remained with the former firm.

In all other instances, a broker cannot legally make any payment to a licensee associated with another principal broker except through that principal broker.

While Principal Broker Smith may not pay the selling share of a commission or pay a finder's fee directly to Jones, a licensee currently associated with Baker Realty, Smith could pay a commission split or referral fee to Allen, a licensee who had earned the fee prior to transferring his license to Baker Realty.

If Dale Richards, an Oregon principal broker, regularly receives information on prospective residential buyers and sellers of real estate from Carolyn Taylor, a commercial broker, he may legally pay her a finder's fee directly if she held an Oregon principal broker's license at the time of the referral. He may not pay her directly if her Oregon broker's license is associated with another principal broker. He may not pay her anything if she did not hold an active real estate license at the time of the referral. However, if she did have the active license at the time of the referral, she could still be paid even if her license is no longer active or valid. (Note: Richards need not disclose the payment of the finder's fee to either the buyer or the seller in the transaction.)

Since a license is required to perform professional real estate activity, payment for real estate activity is always related to when the activity was performed, rather than when the payment was made.

A person who solicited listings prior to obtaining a real estate license would not be entitled to a commission for that activity, even if he obtained a license before the sale closed and commissions were paid.

A broker or property manager may pay a person exempt from the license requirements. For example, a broker may pay an unlicensed person performing property management activities that are permitted under the exemption.

----- COMPENSATION OF AFFILIATED LICENSEES -----

Most often a broker is paid a percentage of the purchase price as a commission, although growing numbers of brokers may now charge a flat fee for various services. Often when a seller specifies a net amount he wishes to receive from a sale, an agent will attempt to arrive at a gross sales price by adding their commission to the net amount desired by the seller.

The seller has been trying to sell the property himself for $100,000. He is willing to list his property with the broker as long as the seller gets $100,000 after the broker's commission is paid. If the broker added a 7% commission to the seller's net amount when calculating the price to ask for the property, this would not be correct, and the seller would not net $100,000 if the property sold for that calculated price. The problem is that the broker has added $7,000 (7% of the $100,000 net) to the net figure. If the property were to sell for $107,000, the broker's commission would be 7% of $107,000, or $7,490. If the broker had written the listing for 7% of the sales price, the seller would net only $99,510 ($107,000-$7,490). If the broker had written it as a net listing, he would get less than 7% of the sales price even if the property sold for the full $107,000.

The correct manner of figuring the price in this situation is to calculate the total amount the seller will want or need after paying only the commission. This amount is the net plus all other expenses. It will be equal to the sales price less the broker's commission. As a percentage it is equal to 100% of the sale price less the commission rate. If the commission were 7%, the amount to the seller would be 93% of the sales price. To calculate the sales price divide the amount the seller gets by the percentage he gets, in this case 93% ($100,000 ÷ 93% = $107,527).

The portion of the principal broker's commission paid to an affiliated licensee will depend entirely on his contract with his principal broker.

Most often, an affiliated licensee is paid a percentage of the brokerage fees received on his transactions. This may range from 50% to 80% of the principal broker's fee.

On the sale of a $300,000 house by a licensee who lists and sells the property, a principal broker may get a 5% commission and the affiliated licensee who listed and sold the property gets 60%. The total principal broker's fee is therefore $15,000 (5 % x $300,000), out of which the affiliated licensee's fee is $9,000 (60% x $15,000).

If the property is listed by one licensee, and sold by another, the share of the commission paid to affiliated licensees is split into a sales portion and listing portion. For example, if the split were half to the licensee who listed the property and half to the one who actually sold it, each licensee would receive half of $9,000 or $4,500. In these transactions, the principal broker pays each affiliated licensee. The commission does not go directly to the licensees to split with each other, as no one but a principal broker may pay a licensee.

Most compensation programs provide for the percentages of the principal broker's fee paid to the affiliated licensee to rise as the licensee's level of production increases during the year. For example, a program may provide for payment of 50% of the commission on principal broker earnings up to $12,000, 60% between $12,001 and $20,000, and 75% above $20,000.

Some companies start the commission scales over each year, while others may start them at a higher level, close to or equal to the prior year's level.

In some companies the affiliated licensee's commissions have been increased to 100% of the principal broker's commission. In these companies the affiliated licensees pay the principal broker a flat fee to cover the brokerage costs of office space, telephone, computers, equipment and supervision, pay their own advertising and marketing costs, and, in return, keep the entire commission earned. One of the benefits to the principal broker is that the monthly fee assures the principal broker of a steady income to cover his costs and to earn a profit. This transfers all of the risks of the real estate business to the associate licensees. Another benefit is that this method attracts and helps keep high-volume producers, as they would earn more under this arrangement than under a split arrangement. In addition, they would be less likely to leave and open up their own offices, since they would then have a greater overhead expense.

The arrangement is legal as long as a principal real estate broker does not use a 100% commission arrangement to evade the principal broker's responsibility to supervise his affiliated licensees and the affiliated licensees do not use the 100% commission arrangement to control the employing broker in a real estate transaction or to act independently of the principal broker.

Offices utilizing the 100% commission plan must meet the same legal requirements as other real estate offices, and the principal broker has the same duty to train and supervise affiliated licensees and review documents prepared by them.

Many companies have tried variations of this basic concept. In some, there is an additional charge per transaction. This enables the principal broker to charge a lower base fee and then collect an additional fee from those who would be able to pay to make up the rest of the amount he needs. In other companies, the base fee is kept low but additional fees are charged for various services the principal broker provides, such as secretarial services. This enables each licensee to have some control over the total amount he will pay the principal broker, but it can create bookkeeping problems and a problem with licensees becoming overly reluctant to incur expenses necessary to make the sales.

Some companies offer affiliated licensees a varying scale of commissions with balancing fees. For example, a company may pay some affiliated licensees 50% and charge no fee, pay some 80% and charge a $500 monthly fee, and pay others 100% and charge a $1,000 monthly fee. This allows affiliated licensees to choose how much of a risk they wish to undertake.

Suit for Commission

A principal real estate broker in Oregon may not bring or maintain any action in the courts for the collection of compensation without proving that he was a licensed broker at the time of the alleged cause of action.

A legal action for collection of compensation for a broker associated with a principal broker may only be brought by the principal broker with whom he was associated at the time of the alleged cause of action. Thus, an associate licensee cannot sue a seller who refuses to pay a commission.

Since only a principal broker or property manager not associated with a broker has a right to claim a commission from a client, an associate licensee of a principal broker may not change or renegotiate the commission in a transaction without the prior approval and written consent of the principal broker. Every listing agreement, buyer agency agreement, or property management agreement is a contract with the principal broker, not with the associated licensee. Only the principal broker can change or renegotiate the commission amount in the employment contract. This is so, even if the associate licensee is an independent contractor and even if the associate licensee is getting 100% of the commission amount at closing.

----- REBATING AND RENEGOTIATING COMMISSIONS -----

As the license law prohibits payment of compensation to any person who is not a real estate licensee, licensed under the license law, a licensee cannot share his commission with his client, the buyer or seller, charitable organizations, other client service providers, etc. This limits, to some extent, demands on earned commissions by clients and customers. However, it also limits the ability of licensees to use rebates and the like to effect transactions and often leads to an inadvertent illegal sharing of real estate commissions, when the licensee is merely trying to bring about a reduction in the commission or to provide extra services.

The following types of violations may surface in the sale agreement, the escrow instructions, closing statements, and/or the listing agreement itself:

- A broker agrees to pay a $400 insurance premium on behalf of the buyer directly from his commission to a homeowner warranty insurance company, a third party vendor of goods or services.
- A listing agent agrees to reduce his commission to accommodate the seller in the transaction by virtue of a credit back of $1,500 of his commission, paid at closing.
- A broker's listing agreement provides that, if the property is not sold in 60 days, the broker agrees to credit the seller $1,000 at closing. In this case, the listing broker is, in effect, improperly sharing $1,000 of a commission.
- An addendum to the sale agreement provided that the "Real estate commission is to be 7%. Agents agree to credit the seller the sum of $1,250 at closing." The closing statement then reflected these disbursements to the seller. In this case, the broker has agreed to reduce his commission in the sale agreement by directly crediting the seller from escrow a sum that effectively reduced the commission rate.

Each of these examples is a violation of the law even though they may not seem serious. The licensee's intent is not to share a commission, but to provide the client with a reduced charge for services. However, the improper structuring of the commission reduction can have negative consequences, including a license suspension.

A licensee will be making an agreement to illegally share a commission when he provides for a direct payment of a portion of his commission to the seller, buyer or any other person, at or after closing. Therefore, any agreement involving a commission should be stated in a document separate from the sale agreement and have the commission reduction applied before closing.

If handled properly, a reduction of a commission charged a seller or buyer can comply with the law. If done improperly, however, it is an illegal rebate. When a broker has an exclusive right-to-sell listing with a seller and the seller wants to net a specific dollar amount, the broker may need to reduce the fixed percentage commission in the listing agreement in order to get the seller the desired net. This would not be rebating a portion of the commission if the broker made the commission amount subject to the seller's desired "net."

One way in which to do this is to agree to renegotiate the commission in the listing agreement prior to closing, at the seller's request. The broker and the seller can agree in the listing contract that the broker's compensation will be a certain amount unless it  appears prior to closing that the seller will not receive the desired "net." In that case, the broker will renegotiate prior to closing to either reduce or defer the commission to provide the seller's desired "net" at closing.

As an alternative, the broker could simply renegotiate the compensation with the seller at any time prior to closing. If it looks like the seller will not receive the desired "net" because of unexpected sales costs or a lower sales price than expected, the broker can renegotiate the compensation with the seller and agree with the seller to take less compensation from the sale.

Some local multiple listing service rules may require that the broker disclose that a listing contract includes a variable rate commission arrangement if the broker agrees to renegotiate the commission in the listing contract. A broker should check with the MLS to see what, if any, disclosure must be made in any offer of cooperation and compensation through the MLS.

Cooperative Transactions

In a **co-op transaction**, the listing broker gets the commission regardless of who sells the property. When he gets his commission, he will pay a portion to the listing licensee. He will pay another portion to the selling broker if he has agreed to cooperate with the selling broker and that broker has an active license. The selling broker then pays a portion to the selling licensee. In practice, the split between brokers is paid by escrow directly to each broker.

For Example	A home sold for $300,000. The listing broker's fee is 5% or $15,000. The listing broker agrees to pay the selling broker 2.25% of the sales price, or $6,750, and will keep 3.75%, or $8,250. If the listing sales associate is to get 50% of the listing broker's $8,250, he would be paid $4,125. If the selling sales associate is to get 60% of the selling broker's $6,750, he would receive $4,050.

An agreement of a listing broker to share a commission with a cooperating broker need not be written. It could be under a written agreement, including an agreement through association with an MLS, or under an oral agreement. Generally, brokers working with buyers as agents of the buyers will receive their compensation from the seller's agents through the MLS offer of compensation and cooperation to buyers' agents. This is the common practice, since a buyer will have limited cash available after the closing to pay the cash for his agent's commission. Lenders, while typically unwilling to finance buyer-paid commissions, are willing to, in effect, finance the buyer's commissions when they are part of the purchase price offered and are paid by the seller through the seller's agent to the buyer's agent.

For Example	A buyer is willing to pay $150,000 for a home if the seller pays the buyer's broker's $5,000 commission. However, if the buyer has to pay the commission directly, the buyer may offer only $140,000 for the house, since he will have to pay the commission and will have fewer funds available to pay closing costs.

The practice of the seller's agent paying the buyer's agent's commission makes it necessary for the brokers to exercise diligence when negotiating fees at the time of offer presentation. These negotiations can lead to commission disputes between brokers when one may claim a right to a commission the other does not believe was deserved, or when the actions of one affect the commission expected by the other.

In a case involving a commission dispute in a co-op transaction, the buyer's agent was to be paid by the seller through the listing broker. The offer was below the listing price, and the seller wanted to lower the commission and retract the offer of a bonus to the selling agent as a condition of accepting an offer at less than full price.

The position of the Agency is that it is legal for the buyer's agent to be paid by the seller and seller's agent. It is also legal for a buyer's agent to receive a selling bonus from the seller for making the sale. In such instances, the seller's agent has a duty to clearly set forth in writing in the listing any conditions to be met by a buyer's agent in order to receive the bonus. The existence of a selling bonus from the seller would constitute a potential conflict of interest for a buyer's agent, as it could cause the agent to make choices that were more in favor of the agent than the buyer. Therefore, when showing property having a selling bonus, the buyer's agent's has a duty to fully disclose to the buyer the existence of the offer of the bonus.

In this case, the listing agent offered a selling bonus to a selling broker through the MLS. The listing agent failed to specify in the MLS, prior to the writing and presentation of an offer, that the selling bonus was contingent upon a full price offer being presented and accepted. When the buyer's agent submitted an offer on behalf of the buyer below the listing price, the listing agent attempted to retract the bonus to be paid to the selling broker. The Agency considered the reduction of the selling agent's fee after the offer had been produced to be a violation of the prohibition against misrepresentation and acting in bad faith. The Agency found nothing wrong with cooperating brokers agreeing to reduce their fees before an offer had been produced or even after an offer had been made in order to put the transaction together. It further determined that any reduction must be accomplished as a written side agreement rather than as a contingency in a counteroffer.

The same would be true if the buyer's agent felt the brokerage fees had to be reduced to enable the transaction to close and submitted an offer on behalf of a buyer contingent on a fee reduction by the seller's agent. This would be improper, as it would interfere with the contract between the seller and the listing agent.

When brokers submit their listings to the multiple listing service they are in effect marketing the listed property to other brokers. This would be considered advertising. In this advertising, they are creating a unilateral contract between the listing broker and the selling broker that produces the buyer. When making the offer of cooperation and compensation to other brokers, whether as a percentage of the sale price or as a flat dollar amount, the selling broker can expect that the amount promised would be paid in the event he produces a ready, willing and able buyer whose offer is accepted by the seller. When the listing agent unilaterally changes the offer after the buyer's agent has written it, this can be considered misrepresentation, false advertising, misleading promises or bad faith, and/or breach of contract.

The Agency takes the position that, when a counteroffer is contingent upon the buyer's agent accepting a reduced fee, this in effect coerces the buyer's agent into accepting the reduced fee in order to represent the buyer's best interests. The buyer's agent's task is to get the best possible price for the buyer, at the best possible terms, on the property selected by the buyer. To avoid violating his fiduciary obligation, he would have to consider the buyer's interest above that of his own in the transaction. If he accepted the reduced fee in order to avoid violating his fiduciary obligation or to avoid drawing the buyer and seller into the conflict between the brokers, he would have likely grounds for filing a case for arbitration.

The time to negotiate fees should be at the time the listing is taken or, if necessary, prior to submission of the offer. If the offer is made and fees need to be adjusted to make the transaction work for the parties, the agents should work toward a mutual agreement. It would be a violation of the license law for one agent to try to impose a new agreement after obtaining the services of another based on false or misleading promises.

Brokers associated with principal brokers must also remember that any fees to be paid or received are accepted or rejected by the principal broker, unless the principal broker's office policy delegates that authority to the associate broker. Therefore, the principal broker should be brought into the negotiating process for advice and approval. This will help to reduce any emotions that may affect the thinking of the associate brokers in working out the problem.

A cooperating broker should not try to persuade the buyer to include a provision where the seller and purchaser will agree that the listing broker will compensate the cooperating broker in an amount in excess of that offered by the listing broker. This would be placing the agent's welfare above that of the buyer. However, if the buyer independently chose to include, or instructed his agent to include the provision in the contract or if the offer stated that the seller, as opposed to the listing broker, would compensate the cooperating broker, this would be acceptable, provided the cooperating broker had not suggested such a provision.

In circumstances where brokers feel they must renegotiate their commissions or splits, the best professional practice is for the listing broker and the cooperating broker to discuss the issue with one another, in the best interest of selling the property and being fair to all parties, and renegotiate the split outside the sales agreement. Forthright discussion will almost always engender cooperation to get the transaction concluded.

Payment to a Broker in Another State or Country

A principal broker may pay a finder's fee or a share of the commission on a cooperative sale to a licensed real estate broker in another state or country that has a law permitting real estate brokers to cooperate with real estate brokers or principal real estate brokers in Oregon. The nonresident broker must not be involved in Oregon in any acts constituting professional real estate activity for which compensation is paid. If a country does not license real estate brokers, the payee must be a citizen or resident of the country and represent that he is in the business of real estate brokerage in the other country. Since Mexico does not license brokers, a citizen or resident of Mexico in the real estate brokerage business there could receive the fee.

Dave has listed a house in Oregon. A California broker comes to Oregon to look at the property and wants to submit an offer on behalf of his client. He also wants a share of Dave's commission. Assuming California does have a law permitting brokers to cooperate with real estate brokers in Oregon, a California broker would be able to share a commission only if he does not conduct in Oregon any acts constituting professional real estate activity. Under the Agency's narrow interpretation of "conduct of professional real estate activity," an out-of-state broker who accompanies a prospective buyer on an inspection trip into Oregon to look at property is considered to be conducting professional real estate activity and, therefore, would have to be licensed in Oregon.

Nonresidential Transactions

For a nonresidential transaction there is some loosening of this rule. An Oregon principal broker may share a commission on a cooperative nonresidential real estate transaction with a person who holds an active real estate license in another state or country and who does come into the state to handle the transaction for his client. **Nonresidential real estate**, in this case, is real property improved or available for improvement by commercial structures or five or more residential dwelling units. This would include vacant land available for improvement with commercial or multi-family structures.

The out-of-state real estate licensee may perform professional real estate activity in Oregon if he and the cooperating Oregon principal broker agree in writing that those acts will be under the supervision and control of the cooperating Oregon principal broker, will comply with all applicable Oregon laws, and the cooperating Oregon principal broker will accompany the out-of-state licensee and the client during any property showings or negotiations conducted in Oregon. All property showings and negotiations regarding the nonresidential real estate located in Oregon must be conducted under the supervision and control of the cooperating Oregon principal broker.

Brain Teaser

Reinforce your understanding of the material by correctly completing the following sentences:

1. A _____ _____ is compensation for finding, referring or recommending a prospective client or customer interested in professional real estate activity.

2. A licensee may pay a finder's fee to a licensed property manager only if the referral relates to property management, _____ or _____.

3. The portion of the principal broker's commission paid to an affiliated licensee will depend entirely on his contract with his _____ _____.

4. Generally, brokers working with buyers as agents of the buyers will receive their compensation from the _____ _____.

Brain Teaser Answers

1. A **finder's fee** is compensation for finding, referring or recommending a prospective client or customer interested in professional real estate activity.

2. A licensee may pay a finder's fee to a licensed property manager only if the referral relates to property management, **rental** or **leasing**.

3. The portion of the principal broker's commission paid to an affiliated licensee will depend entirely on his contract with his **principal broker**.

4. Generally, brokers working with buyers as agents of the buyers will receive their compensation from the **seller's agents**.

Review — Oregon Compensation

This lesson explores issues relating to payment of compensation to licensed and unlicensed persons in a real estate transaction.

A real estate licensee cannot offer, promise, allow, give, pay or rebate, directly or indirectly, any part or share of his commission or compensation arising or accruing from any real estate transaction or pay a finder's fee to any person who is not a real estate licensee licensed under the license law. A finder's fee is compensation for finding, referring or recommending a prospective client or customer interested in professional real estate activity.

A broker may pay a finder's fee to a licensed property manager only if the referral relates to property management, rental or leasing. On the other hand, a licensed property manager could pay a referral fee, a finder's fee, or a commission to a sole practitioner broker, principal broker, broker (through the principal broker) or other property manager for finding a prospective renter for one of the property manager's rental properties, or for referral of owners for property management services, because they are authorized to engage in property management activity for a fee.

Sharing Commissions
A principal broker may pay a commission or fee to a licensee who is currently associated with him, or who had been associated with him at the time the commission or fee was earned, even if that person is associated with another broker or has an inactive license or an expired license at the time of payment. In all other instances, a broker cannot legally make any payment to a licensee associated with another principal broker except through that principal broker.

The portion of the principal broker's commission paid to an affiliated licensee will depend entirely on his contract with his principal broker. 100% commission offices must meet the same legal requirements as other real estate offices, and the principal broker has the same duty to train and supervise affiliated licensees and review documents prepared by them.

A legal action for collection of compensation for a broker associated with a principal broker may only be brought or maintained by the principal broker with whom he was associated at the time the cause of action arose. Thus, an associate licensee cannot sue a seller who refuses to pay a commission.

Rebating and Renegotiating Commissions
A licensee cannot share his commission with his client, the buyer or seller, charitable organizations, other client service providers, and so on. Therefore, any agreement involving a commission should be stated in a document separate from the sales agreement and have the commission reduction applied before closing.

Cooperative Transactions
An agreement of a listing broker to share a commission with a cooperating broker need not be written. The Real Estate Agency takes the position that when a counteroffer is contingent upon

the buyer's agent accepting a reduced fee, this in effect coerces the buyer's agent into accepting the reduced fee in order to represent the buyer's best interests. In circumstances where brokers feel they must renegotiate their commissions or splits, the best professional practice is for the listing broker and the cooperating broker to discuss the issue with one another in the best interest of selling the property and, being fair to all parties, renegotiate the split outside the sales agreement.

A sole principal broker or principal broker may pay a finder's fee or a share of the commission on a cooperative sale to a licensed real estate broker in another state or country that has a law permitting real estate brokers to cooperate with real estate brokers or principal real estate brokers in Oregon. The nonresident broker cannot conduct in Oregon any acts constituting professional real estate activity for which compensation is paid.

An Oregon sole principal broker or principal broker may share a commission on a cooperative nonresidential real estate transaction with a person who holds an active real estate license in another state or country and who does come into the state to handle the transaction for his client.

Nonresidential Transactions

For a nonresidential transaction there is some loosening of this rule. An Oregon principal broker may share a commission on a cooperative nonresidential real estate transaction with a person who holds an active real estate license in another state or country and who does come into the state to handle the transaction for his client. **Nonresidential real estate**, in this case, is real property improved or available for improvement by commercial structures or five or more residential dwelling units. This would include vacant land available for improvement with commercial or multi-family structures.

The out-of-state real estate licensee may perform acts in Oregon that constitute professional real estate activity if he and the cooperating Oregon sole practitioner broker or principal broker agree in writing that the acts constituting professional real estate activity conducted in Oregon will be under the supervision and control of the cooperating Oregon sole practitioner broker, will comply with all applicable Oregon laws, and the cooperating Oregon sole practitioner broker or principal broker accompanies the out-of-state licensee and the client during any property showings or negotiations conducted in Oregon.

Oregon Licensing

Overview

This lesson explores the requirements for holding a real estate license, which allows the licensee to perform certain activities. The roles of the Real Estate Agency, Real Estate Commissioner and Real Estate Board are detailed. Discussion of procedures to obtain and renew a license concludes the lesson.

Objectives

Upon completion of this lesson, the student should be able to:

1. Identify the real estate activities that require a license and those that do not require licensure.
2. Explain requirements for real estate licenses in the sales of businesses.
3. Explain the significant differences between a real estate broker, principal broker and licensed property manager.
4. Describe the powers and duties of the Real Estate Agency, Real Estate Commissioner, and Real Estate Board.
5. Describe the general licensing requirements for principal brokers and brokers.
6. Describe the general license application procedures for principal brokers and brokers.
7. Explain the continuing education requirements for licensees.
8. Describe when a transaction is a securities transaction.

Types of Licenses

----- LICENSE REQUIRED -----

Oregon state statutes, enacted by the Oregon State Legislature, are called the **Oregon Revised Statutes** (or ORS). One portion of the statutes is the Oregon Real Estate License Law. This is contained in **Chapter 696** (referred to as ORS 696). ORS 696 establishes:

- when a real estate license is needed;
- the requirements for obtaining and keeping a license;
- conduct which may lead to disciplinary action against a licensee; and
- procedures for enforcement of the law, including the types of disciplinary action which may be taken.

Rules to implement the law are created by the **Real Estate Commissioner** and are contained in Oregon Administrative Rules Section 863.

ORS 696 requires that a person have a real estate license in order to:

- engage in or carry on professional real estate activity.
- engage in, carry on, advertise or purport to engage in or carry on professional real estate activity.
- act in the capacity of a real estate licensee.

One act or transaction of professional real estate activity is sufficient to constitute engaging in professional real estate activity. Therefore, to perform or attempt to perform just one transaction, a person would need to have a real estate license. Furthermore, the status of the license must be active; it cannot be inactive.

Professional Real Estate Activity

"**Professional real estate activity**" is defined in the statute as any of the following actions, when engaged in for another and for compensation or with the intention or in the expectation or upon the promise of receiving or collecting compensation:

- Any person who sells, exchanges, purchases, rents or leases real estate (e.g., a broker or leasing agent).
- Any person who offers to sell, exchange, purchase, rent or lease real estate. Therefore, a person who offers to place ads in the newspaper or on the Internet or tells people he will perform professional real estate activity would need a license.
- Any person who negotiates, offers, attempts or agrees to negotiate the sale, exchange, purchase, rental or leasing of real estate. A person must be licensed to render services in the negotiation for transfer of an interest in real estate.
- Any person who lists, offers, attempts or agrees to list real estate for sale. A person would need to be licensed to accept a listing to sell a farm or home for compensation.

- Any person who offers, attempts or agrees:
  - to perform or provide a competitive market analysis or letter opinion; or
  - to represent a taxpayer in a small claims procedure in Tax Court, or in a conference or proceeding relating to property taxes before a tax court magistrate or the Department of Revenue, or in a petition to the board of property tax appeals; or
  - to give an opinion in any administrative or judicial proceeding regarding the value of real estate for taxation. However, this activity, when performed by a state-certified appraiser or state-licensed appraiser, is not considered professional real estate activity under the terms of the license law, so those appraisers do not need to obtain real estate licenses.
- Any person who auctions, offers, attempts or agrees to auction real estate. An auctioneer can auction real estate only if holding a real estate license.
- Any person who purports to be engaged in the business of buying, selling, exchanging, renting or leasing real estate. It is not necessary for a person to actually engage in unlicensed activity to be stopped. It is illegal for persons to claim that they are in the real estate business and, as a result take money from people, unless they are licensed.
- Any person who assists or directs in the procuring of prospects, calculated to result in the sale, exchange, leasing or rental of real estate. Therefore, an unlicensed person cannot receive a finder's fee or referral fee for soliciting prospects for a relative or neighbor who was licensed. A property owner or real estate agent may pay licensed persons a finder's fee or referral fee to find prospective buyers, but he may not pay such a fee to an unlicensed person.
- Any person who assists or directs in the negotiation or closing of any transaction calculated or intended to result in the sale, exchange, leasing or rental of real estate. Unlicensed persons cannot be paid for helping negotiate for an owner.
- Any person who advises, counsels, consults or analyzes in connection with real estate values, sales or dispositions, including dispositions through eminent domain procedures. (This does not apply to persons whose counsel involves analyzing or advising of permissible land use alternatives, environmental impact, building and use permit procedures, or demographic market studies.) A person would need a license to charge a consultation fee to a seller for advice on marketing real property.
- Any person who advises, counsels, consults or analyzes in connection with the acquisition or sale of real estate by an entity whose purpose is investment in real estate.
- Any person who performs real estate marketing activity as or for a licensed real estate marketing organization (REMO).

- Any person who engages in management of rental real estate. A person needs a license to market rental property owned by others (i.e., assist in procuring prospective tenants for their rental property or collect rent) for a fee. However, there are some major exemptions from this requirement.
- Any person who buys, sells, offers to buy or sell or otherwise deals in options on real estate. This means a person cannot engage in the business of soliciting options on property as an alternative to soliciting listings on property. When soliciting listings, a person is attempting to have the right to earn a commission for a sale. When dealing in options, a person attempts to control the sale of a property for a specified period. An optionee can resell an option, the right to purchase, at a higher price and keep the difference as profit, or he could exercise the option and then sell the property at a higher price, again making a profit.

For Example	Smith wishes to sell her property for $200,000. She anticipates that if she lists it, it might cost her $14,000 in commissions, so she would net $186,000. Jake, an unlicensed person, offers her $2,000 for a 120-day option to purchase at the $186,000. If Smith accepts, she is guaranteed the $2,000 even if Jake does not exercise the option. Once Smith accepts, Jake attempts to find a buyer who will pay more than $2,000 for the option, or who will pay $200,000 for the property, just as if he had a listing. If he finds a buyer for anything over $2,000 for the option or for more than $188,000 for the property, he makes a profit. If he sells the property for $200,000 he comes out almost the same as if he had a listing. The law considers such dealings in options to be an attempt to evade the requirements of the law.

The term "**real estate**" as used in the law applies not just to real property but to every interest or estate in real property, including "leaseholds and licenses to use, such as timeshare estates and timeshare licenses, whether corporeal or incorporeal, whether freehold or nonfreehold, whether held separately or in common with others and whether the real property is situated in Oregon or elsewhere." Therefore, professional real estate activity requiring an Oregon real estate license would include transactions negotiated in Oregon, relating to real property located elsewhere, e.g., in Washington. It would also include transactions involving the lease or transfer of a leasehold interest and transactions relating to the sale of timeshare licenses, campground memberships, mineral rights, air rights, and other interests in real property.

Manufactured Homes

Based on this definition of real estate, some manufactured (mobile) home sale transactions and some sales of businesses may require a real estate license. A **manufactured home** is a structure or trailer designed to be transported or used on a highway. It is capable of being used as a human dwelling or for a business, office or commercial purpose. If the manufactured home and the land on which it is located are owned by the same person and are to be sold as one unit in the same transaction, the agent must have a real estate license, as the manufactured home in such an instance is considered real property. The transaction would be treated the same as any other real estate transaction, with the exception that, if the manufactured home is still titled as a vehicle, it may involve financing procedures and practices that are different than those used in real property transactions. The licensee would need to be certain the status of the title to the structure is disclosed to the buyer and that the financing is handled appropriately.

On the other hand, if the manufactured home is to be sold separately from the land, whether the land is owned by the owner of the manufactured home or the manufactured home is located on a rental space, the manufactured home is considered personal property. Therefore, the person negotiating the sale of a manufactured home on a rental space in a manufactured home facility would not need a real estate license; he would need a Manufactured Structures Dealer's (MSD) license issued by the Finance and Corporate Securities Division of the Department of Consumer and Business Services. If a manufactured structure is sold separate from the sale of the land, this is considered a personal property transaction and requires an MSD license. The sale of a manufactured structure and land in a single transaction is a real estate transaction and requires a real estate license (but not an MSD license).

Responsibility for maintaining ownership and siting information for manufactured structures lies with **Building Codes Division** (BCD). Most transactions involving buying, moving, or otherwise changing the status of a manufactured home takes place at the county assessor's office, which acts on behalf of the division.

Businesses

In the sale of **businesses**, the license requirement applies when there is a transfer of ownership of the real property on which the business is located or a transfer of a leasehold interest in the real property on which the business is located. Therefore, when a business is offered and sold with transfer or ownership or a lease  of the underlying real estate interest as a package, the license law would apply, as it defines real estate as "including leaseholds and licenses to use, as well as any and every interest or estate in real property, whether corporeal or incorporeal, whether freehold or nonfreehold, whether held separately or in common with others." There is no requirement for a real estate license to engage in a sale of a business when only personal property is involved, i.e., inventory, client and customer lists, goodwill, etc. Therefore, the real estate license is not needed by persons who sell law or accounting practices when the purchaser will operate in a different location.

Compensation

Activities are considered professional real estate activity when they are engaged in for another and for compensation or with the intention or in the expectation or upon the promise of receiving or collecting compensation. **Compensation** includes any fee (e.g., referral fee, finder's fee, management fee), commission, salary, money or valuable consideration for services rendered or to be rendered. It also includes the promise of consideration, whether the payment is contingent (e.g., on the transaction actually taking place or on the dollar amount of the transaction) or otherwise. Therefore, the license requirement applies when a person accepts anything of value (dinner, weekend at the coast, etc.) for these services, regardless of what it may be called and whether it is a set amount, an hourly fee or a percentage of a transaction price. It even applies when a person performs these activities expecting to receive compensation or based on a promise of receiving compensation, but does not actually receive it.

----- TYPES OF LICENSES -----

In Oregon, there are three types of real estate licenses:
1. Real estate broker
2. Principal real estate broker
3. Real estate property manager

Broker

A person with a real estate **broker** license is authorized to engage in all professional real estate activity as a broker associated with a principal real estate broker.

A broker is not permitted to engage in professional real estate activity independent of a principal broker's supervision and control. He may engage in professional real estate activity only in association with a principal real estate broker, licensed to and working only as the agent of the principal broker. A broker, for at least the first three years, must be associated with a principal broker. During that time, the principal broker is responsible for the training and supervision of the broker. After three years, the broker can continue to be licensed as a broker associated with and under the supervision of a principal broker or can become licensed as a principal broker.

Principal Broker

A **principal broker** is a real estate broker who is also authorized to engage in professional real estate activity and is qualified and authorized to employ, engage or otherwise supervise other real estate licensees (principal brokers, brokers and property managers) who are associated with him, act only as his agents, and are subject to his supervision and training. He may conduct business with other principal brokers and enter into contracts to have other brokers, principal brokers and property managers associate with him.

A principal broker may conduct real estate activity in his own name or under a business name registered with the Commissioner, with sole supervision of and control over all clients' funds, clients' trust accounts and the maintenance of adequate records for all professional real estate activity conducted on his behalf. He may conduct sales activity with one or more real estate brokers associated with him and/or conduct property management activity with one or more real estate brokers or licensed real estate property managers associated with him, provided he supervises and controls all of the real estate activities.

Property Manager

The real estate **property manager** license restricts the licensee to only one aspect of professional real estate activity: management of rental real estate. This license may be considered a broker license limited to property management.

Note the following distinctions between the three licenses:

Broker and principal broker licenses authorize the licensee to engage in every type of activity considered to be professional real estate activity (i.e., sales, consulting, property management, etc.). However, a broker must work under the supervision of a principal broker. While a principal real estate broker may employ, engage and otherwise supervise the professional activities of real estate brokers or principal real estate brokers, a real estate broker may not. Any real estate broker who is operating as an administrative or managerial supervisor for one or more other real estate brokers must be licensed as a principal real estate broker.

A licensed property manager may immediately operate independently, without a principal broker's supervision. If he does so, he may work alone or with other licensed property managers or he may contract with and supervise other licensed property managers. Alternatively, he may choose to be associated with a principal broker or another property manager.

----- EXEMPTIONS -----

ORS 696 provides that a number of persons who engage in real estate transactions are not required to have a license.

Any general partner for a domestic or foreign limited partnership duly registered and operating within Oregon is exempt from the law while engaging in the sale of limited partnership interests and while engaging in the acquisition, sale, exchange, lease, transfer or management of the real estate of the limited partnership. Therefore, a general partner does not need to be licensed to engage in a real estate transaction for the limited partnership he manages. Such a person is regulated by securities law, and to avoid unnecessary duplication of regulating efforts, he is exempted from the real estate license law. On the other hand, a limited partner in a limited partnership who is acting under a separate, written property management agreement to rent the real property of the limited partnership on a part-time basis, or who is engaging in the purchase or sale of real estate for the limited partnership, would need a real estate license to do so legally.

The law exempts a person performing an act of professional real estate activity under order of a court.

It also exempts a person acting in his official capacity as a receiver, a conservator, a trustee in bankruptcy, a personal representative or a trustee, or a regular salaried employee of the trustee, acting under a trust agreement, deed of trust or will. Therefore, a personal representative of the estate of a deceased person, such as the executor of a will or an administrator appointed by a court in probate proceedings, may deal in estate property, and manage it, advertise it and negotiate the sale of the property without a real estate license. A trustee may conduct a trustee's sale to foreclose a trust deed without a real estate license.

Real Estate-Related Jobs

The law also exempts from licensure persons whose business or jobs are real estate related but are not of the same nature as real estate brokerage.

A financial institution or trust company is exempt when acting as attorney-in-fact under a duly executed power of attorney from the owner or purchaser authorizing real estate activity, if the power of attorney is recorded in the office of the county clerk for the county in which the real estate to be sold, leased or exchanged is located.

The state, counties and cities acquire, maintain and dispose of their own real estate. The law exempts from licensing a salaried employee of the State of Oregon, or any of its political subdivisions, engaging in professional real estate activity as a part of his employment. As a result, a Department of Veteran's Affairs (DVA) employee may, without a license, sell properties taken back by the DVA through foreclosure. An investment adviser, registered under the Investment Advisers Act of 1940, need not have a real estate license to render real estate investment services for the office of the State Treasurer or the Oregon Investment Council.

Also exempted from licensing is a person, or an employee of the person, selling or leasing cemetery lots, parcels or units while engaged in the disposition of human bodies.

The law also exempts a membership camping contract broker or salesperson when engaged in the sale of membership camping contracts. However, such a person must be registered with the Real Estate Agency (the Agency).

Lodging

The law exempts all those who arrange rental of transient lodging at hotels and inns. Transient lodging includes room rentals on a daily or weekly basis for a period of occupancy of less than 30 consecutive days.

This exemption applies to any hotelkeeper or innkeeper, while in the course of business as a hotelkeeper or innkeeper, as well as to any hotel representative, while in the course of business as a hotel representative, in arranging for compensation, the rental of transient lodging at a hotel or inn. A **hotel representative** is a person who provides reservations or sale services to independent hotels, airlines, steamship companies and government tourist agencies.

The law exempts any common carrier while in the course of business as a common carrier in arranging, for compensation, the rental of transient lodging at a hotel or inn. A **common carrier** is a person who transports, or purports to be willing to transport persons, for hire, compensation or consideration by rail, motor vehicle, boat or aircraft from place to place.

The law exempts any travel agent who, in the course of business as a travel agent, for compensation, arranges the rental of transient lodging at a hotel or inn. A **travel agent** is a person, or an employee of that person, who is regularly engaged in the business of representing and selling travel services to the public directly and/or indirectly through other travel agents.

As a result of these exemptions, hotel clerks do not need licenses to rent rooms, and travel agents, airlines and railroad companies may offer travel packages that include hotel or inn lodging without real estate licenses. However, those who might perform rental service at places other than hotels or inns or independent of the hotel or inn, or rent lodging for longer than 30 days might need a real estate license if not otherwise qualified for an exemption.

Professionals

Certain professionals are exempt when performing services in performance of their professions. An attorney at law may render services in the  performance of duties as an attorney at law. Therefore, he may assist his client in the negotiation of a real estate transaction and draft and review documents and provide legal advice. However, he may not use his license to engage in the business of buying and selling real estate for others.

A registered professional engineer or architect is exempt when rendering services in performance of their duties as a professional engineer or architect.

A professional forester or farm manager may engage in property management activities on forest or farmland, when those activities are incidental to the non-real estate duties involving overall management of forest or farm resources.

Exempt if Unlicensed, but Subject to Law if Licensed

While some persons are exempt from the need for a real estate license to perform various real estate activities under specified conditions, they may still be subject to various provisions of the license law and administrative rules and regulations in performing real estate transactions if they do hold a real estate license. This means they would be subject to recordkeeping requirements, advertising requirements, and supervision requirements imposed by the law.

A license is not needed for a nonlicensed person or his regular full-time employee to, as a **consultant**, analyze or advise as to permissible land use alternatives, environmental impact, building and use permit procedures, or demographic market studies. However, such a person would need to be licensed to handle any transactional negotiations for the transfer of an interest in real estate.

A nonlicensed person acting as a paid fiduciary whose real estate activity is limited to negotiating or closing a transaction to obtain the services of a real estate licensee, is exempt. A nonlicensed person is also exempt while acting as a fiduciary under a court order, without regard to whether the court order specifically authorizes real estate activity.

A nonlicensed person who wants to engage in real estate transactions for himself (i.e., transferring or acquiring any interest in real estate owned or to be owned by that person) is also exempt, except for a person dealing in options. Therefore, a property owner buying or selling a home or investment property or a builder acquiring land and selling his own buildings need not have a real estate license. However, if that person had a real estate license when he transferred or acquired an interest in real estate he owned or was to own, he would have to disclose his license status, conduct the transaction under the supervision and control of his principal broker, and act up to the standards of competency and trustworthiness required of a licensee when dealing with any party in a real estate transaction.

Attorney-in-Fact

Various nonlicensed persons are exempt when acting as an attorney-in-fact under a duly executed power of attorney.

One of these is a nonlicensed person acting as an **attorney-in-fact** for an owner or purchaser. The attorney-in-fact may supervise the closing of or performance of a contract for the sale, leasing or exchanging of real estate, if the power of attorney was:

- duly executed and in compliance with the law before July 1, 2002, or
- recorded in the office of the recording officer for the county in which the real estate is located, specifically describes the real estate, and is not used as a device to engage in professional real estate activity without obtaining the necessary real estate license.

Another exemption applies to a nonlicensed person acting as an attorney-in-fact under a power of attorney, in which he is the spouse of the principal, or the child, grandchild, parent, grandparent, sibling, aunt, uncle, niece or nephew of the principal or his spouse. Under this scenario, he is authorized to conduct real estate activity so long as the power of attorney is recorded in the county in which the real estate to be sold, leased or exchanged is located.

Since these exemptions apply only to nonlicensed persons acting under a power of attorney, a licensed person acting under a power of attorney would have to disclose he was licensed and have the transaction conducted through the principal broker.

Nonlicensed Employees

Certain nonlicensed employees are exempt when performing real estate-related activities for their employer.

A nonlicensed regular full-time employee of a single owner of real estate may be exempt from the licensing requirement when performing real estate activity for the employer.

> **NOTE:** An owner is considered a single owner whether title to the real estate is vested in severalty or in more than one person by tenancy by the entirety, tenancy in common or by survivorship.

The exemption would not apply to a person employed full time for two weeks by one owner and then employed a number of weeks for another owner. In that instance, he would not be a regular full-time employee. Nor could the employee be exempt if he were employed on a regular basis by two or more employers at the same time.

<table>
<tr><td>For Example</td><td>If three people own a property as tenants in common, they are considered a single owner. A person employed by the three tenants in common could be exempt from the law if he is a regular full-time employee and not also employed by other property owners.</td></tr>
</table>

The nonlicensed employee is exempt if the principal activity of his job involves real estate activity for his employer, but his employer's principal activity or business is not the sale, exchange, lease option or acquisition of real estate.

<table>
<tr><td>For Example</td><td>An unlicensed employee of an oil company can negotiate the purchase and sale of real estate or manage the leases on service station sites for the company, since the company's principal activity is not buying and selling real estate. Since the employee must be a regular full-time employee, the employee would not be exempt if he were hired only for the purpose of locating one parcel.</td></tr>
</table>

It is important to note that this exemption is worded so that a nonlicensed employee of a builder or developer could not negotiate the acquisition or sale of the builder's property, since the sale of real property is the builder's principal activity. Therefore, builders must either sell their property themselves or through licensed real estate agents. This assures that persons representing the builder have had to satisfy requirements for competency and trustworthiness to become licensed.

A nonlicensed employee is also exempt if his real estate activity involves the real estate of the employer and is incidental to the employee's normal, non-real estate activities. Therefore, unlicensed employees of a builder could get involved in a transaction for the builder when the involvement is incidental to their normal functions, such as a construction supervisor occasionally letting people into houses under construction.

Also exempt is a nonlicensed regular fulltime employee of a single nonlicensed corporation, partnership, association or individual owner of real property acting for the employer/owner in the rental or management of the real property. The employee may not be involved in the sale, exchange, lease option or purchase of the real property. This exemption allows a person to act without a license as the property manager hired by a condominium owners association or as a resident manager of one or more apartment buildings for one owner.

However, a regular full time employee of a single owner of real estate who could have bought, sold and managed real estate for his employer if he did not have a license, would have to arrange for the activity to be conducted under a principal broker's supervision until he was eligible to perform professional real estate activity as a principal broker, if he had a real estate license. Such a person could not act as a property manager for more than

 one owner at a time and could not perform any other professional real estate activity for the owner without an active real estate license.

The license law would also apply to a licensed regular full time employee of an owner in the rental or management of real estate. A person employed as a resident manager would not need a real estate license. However, if he became a licensed broker, he would be required to have the owner enter into a property management agreement with his principal broker and have all of the resident manager activity conducted on behalf of and supervised by a principal broker. If such a person became licensed as a real estate property manager, he would have to have the property owner enter into a property management agreement with the property management firm and handle all of the activity as resident manager under his property manager license.

The law also exempts a nonlicensed individual employed by a principal real estate broker or property manager and acting as a manager for real estate so long as his real estate activity is limited to negotiating rental or lease agreements, checking tenant and credit references, physically maintaining the real estate, conducting tenant relations, collecting the rent, supervising the premises managers (i.e., resident managers), and discussing financial matters relating to management of the real estate with the owner.

Therefore, a principal broker could hire unlicensed on-site managers and unlicensed employees to supervise the site managers, but not to supervise licensed activities. Unlicensed employees could handle all activity relating to tenants, including soliciting them, screening them, negotiating leases and rental agreements, collecting rent, handling tenant problems, handling repairs, etc. They could not solicit new property management business, and they could not negotiate or sign property management agreements with owners.

Property management agreements may be negotiated and signed by the principal broker or, on behalf of the principal broker, by a broker or property manager licensed under the principal broker. They may also be negotiated and signed by a property manager licensed independently. An employee of a property manager, acting for the property manager as a resident manager or otherwise, may not negotiate or sign a property management agreement with a property owner.

The law also allows a nonlicensed person to receive compensation for referral of a new tenant to a real estate licensee acting as the property manager for a residential building or facility while that person resides in the building or facility or within six months after termination of his tenancy. However, a licensed person receiving a referral fee for a tenant in the building would have to have that fee paid to his principal broker.

The law also allows a nonlicensed person to receive compensation for giving an opinion in an administrative or judicial proceeding regarding the value of real estate for taxation or for representing taxpayer in a tax appeal or hearing. This is because such a person would need to be licensed or certified as an appraiser; a real estate licensee is allowed to do so as an exemption under the appraisal license law. However, licensed person giving assistance in a tax proceeding or appeal would have to have the fee or compensation paid to the licensee's principal broker.

License Requirements

----- REAL ESTATE AGENCY AND COMMISSIONER -----

The state agency that issues real estate licenses and enforces the provisions of the Real Estate License Law is called the **Real Estate Agency** (the Agency). The Agency has the following authority:

- To provide Oregon real estate licensees printed matter which is helpful or educational or proper for their guidance and welfare.
- To make and enforce reasonable rules necessary to administer and enforce the law. These rules and regulations have the force and effect of law, so a violation of an Agency rule is treated the same as a violation of the law passed by the legislature.

The Agency is under the supervision and control of an administrator, the Real Estate Commissioner (the Commissioner). The Commissioner is appointed by the Governor. He is responsible for the performance of the duties imposed on the Agency, but may delegate authority to exercise those duties. Any act performed in the Commissioner's name and by his authority is considered to be an official act of the Commissioner.

The Commissioner may assign staff in the Agency to perform any duties he considers necessary to advance education and research in connection with the education of real estate licensees, including the publication of the *Oregon Real Estate News-Journal* and other educational printed matter for licensees.

The Commissioner has authority to conduct investigations and hold hearings relating to applicants for real estate licenses and to possible violations of the law and rules. If any person fails to comply with a request for information or a subpoena or refuses to testify in a legal or administrative proceeding, the Commissioner may take action to compel obedience.

Except for records of open investigations, all records kept in the Commissioner's office are open to public inspection.

All money, fees and charges (e.g., license and exam fees, civil penalties, etc.) collected or received by the Agency are deposited in the Real Estate Account in the general fund of the State Treasury for use in paying the Agency's expenses.

Only the state may require or issue a real estate license or charge a fee for licensing or regulation of real estate licensees. However, a county, city or town may collect a business license fee and levy a tax based on the amount of business conducted by any licensee or firm within its jurisdiction. Most cities and counties do charge a fee for a business permit to operate in that jurisdiction. The fee can be imposed on a principal broker but not on a real estate broker who engages in professional real estate activity only as an agent of a principal broker.

----- REAL ESTATE BOARD -----

A **Real Estate Board** is established within the Agency. It is an advisory board, and its purpose is to:

- inquire into the needs of Oregon real estate licensees, the functions of the Agency and its business policy.
- confer with and advise the Governor as to how the Agency may best serve the state and the licensees.
- recommend and suggest policy to the Agency.
- recommend whether or not to grant waivers of license requirements, requested by license applicants.

The Board also reviews and makes recommendations regarding proposals of the Agency to adopt, amend or repeal rules concerning real estate licensees. The Agency must consider these recommendations and publish any written comments submitted by the Board as part of the statement of need for the rule.

----- LICENSE QUALIFICATIONS -----

Any License
To qualify for any real estate license, an applicant must at the time of the application:

- have a high school diploma, GED certificate or the international equivalent.
- be a least 18 years of age.
- complete his required education.
- submit a license application and application fee (if the application is for renewal of a license, in addition to the application fee, the applicant must pay any unpaid money owed to the Agency).
- pass any required licensing exam.
- submit a background check application and fingerprints to show he is trustworthy and competent to conduct professional real estate activity in a manner that protects the public interest. Past criminal convictions or even a license revocation would not automatically prevent a person from obtaining a license, if there is evidence that the applicant could be considered trustworthy at the time of application.

Residency
An applicant for an Oregon real estate license need not be a resident or a citizen of Oregon. An individual who is not a resident of Oregon can obtain a license under the same terms as an Oregon resident, or under certain circumstances, he can obtain an Oregon nonresident license.

A **nonresident license** may be obtained by an individual who resides in and is licensed to actively engage in professional real estate activity in another state or country, if that state or country will:

- license Oregon brokers under terms and conditions similar to those prescribed in Oregon law.
- assist the Commissioner in reviewing real estate transactions and management of rental real estate conducted by nonresident licensees.

A license issued to a nonresident licensee will contain the name and business address of the nonresident broker under whose license he works and will be mailed to that broker at that address. All advertising used by such a licensee must contain the name and business address of the nonresident broker.

A nonresident license authorizes the Agency to inspect and examine all transaction escrow records, trust account records and other records of professional real estate activity conducted in Oregon by the licensee, wherever they are maintained, and upon request the licensee must produce them at the Agency's office.

Aside from these provisions, the application, fees, license terms, license application processing and renewal, license transfer, and all other conditions and requirements of licensure are the same as for resident licensees.

The Commissioner may enter into reciprocity agreements with other states or countries, where necessary, to permit Oregon real estate licensees to obtain licenses in such other states or countries.

Every licensee must maintain on file with the Agency a current mailing address. A licensee must notify the Agency by use of the eLicense system within 10 days of a change of mailing or email address.

In addition to these requirements, an applicant may need to satisfy course, examination and/or experience requirements depending on the license or license status for which he is applying.

Brokers

A real estate broker's educational **courses** consist of 150 hours of coursework in the following subjects:

- Real Estate Law (30 hours)
- Real Estate Finance (30 hours)
- Oregon Real Estate Practice (30 hours)
- Contracts (15 hours)
- Agency (15 hours)
- Property Management (10 hours)
- Real Estate Brokerage (20 hours)

Courses offered to satisfy these requirements must:

- be designed according to the Guidelines for Oregon Private Real Estate Schools and Instructional Guidelines.
- be approved by the Commissioner.
- include a final examination requiring a passing score of at least 75% as evidence of successful completion.

The **license exam** is a two-part exam:

- One part covers national or general real estate matters. It has 150 questions, with the number of questions for each topic roughly matching the number of hours for each course. This means there should be about 30 questions relating to law, 30 relating to finance, etc.
- The other part covers real estate specifically related to Oregon. It has 50 questions, with 30 relating to regulation of licensees and 20 relating to other Oregon laws relating to real estate.

The applicant must pass both parts of the exam with a score of at least 75%. If he passes only one part, the results of the part passed are valid for a year, and he can become licensed by passing the other part within the year. If he does not pass the other part within a year, he would have to retake the entire exam.

If he does not have a license issued within one year of passing both parts of the license exam, the exam would have to be retaken.

During the period between passing the license exam and having a license issued, the applicant is not considered licensed. He cannot engage in any professional real estate activity for others, but can engage in personal transactions without being subject to any provisions of the license law relating to disclosure of licensing or recordkeeping.

In order to have a license issued, the broker applicant must designate the principal broker with whom he will be associated. He cannot be associated with more than one principal broker during the same period of time.

Principal Brokers

To qualify to be a principal broker, an applicant must have three years of active experience as a real estate licensee in Oregon or elsewhere, or equivalent real estate-related experience. An applicant with experience based wholly or partially upon an active real estate license held in another state must furnish with the application a certification of active licensing from that state's licensing agency.

However, an applicant may petition the Board for a principal broker license after holding an active broker license for at least:

- one year, with a degree in real estate from a four-year college or university, in a curriculum approved by the Commissioner.
- two years, with an associate degree in an approved real estate technology curriculum from a two-year community college (and a completed brokerage administration and sales supervision course if applying for a principal broker license).

A principal broker applicant must:

- successfully complete an Agency-approved 40-hour course in Brokerage Administration and Sales Supervision.
- pass a 48-question principal broker license exam.
- designate and register a place of business and/or a business name under which he will be conducting professional real estate activity or identify the principal broker with whom he will be licensed.

An individual eligible to be a principal broker has a choice of:

- remaining licensed as a broker associated with a principal broker.
- becoming licensed as the principal broker of his own firm.
- becoming licensed as a principal broker associated with a principal broker.

Property Manager License

To qualify for a real estate property manager license, an applicant must:

- submit his license application and fee.
- successfully complete a 60-hour property management course covering legal aspects of real estate, real estate property management and accounting, bookkeeping and trust accounting practices.
- pass a 100-question real estate property manager license examination.
- provide fingerprints.
- indicate the name under which he will operate or identify the property manager or principal broker with whom he will be associated.

----- LICENSE RENEWAL -----

All licenses are issued for a two-year term expiring at the end of the licensee's birth month the second year after issuance.

For Example	Joe Smith has a birth date of March 3, and is issued a license on Sept. 28, 2009. His initial license will expire March 31, 2011. It then may be renewed indefinitely every two years. Each license received upon renewal will expire March 31, every other year.

The licensee must submit a completed renewal application and a renewal fee to the Commissioner on or before the license expiration date. The fee for an active license is the same as the initial license fee, $230. The fee to renew a license as an inactive license is $110.

Prior to his first renewal of an active license, a broker licensee must complete a 30-hour Advanced Real Estate Practice course.

For any active license renewal after the first, a licensee must complete, during the preceding two license years, 30 clock-hours of continuing education from certified course providers within eligible course topics established by the Real Estate Agency. The 30 hours must include a three-hour Law & Rule required course approved by the Real Estate Board.

----- SECURITIES -----

A real estate license does not authorize a person to engage in securities transactions involving real estate. Transactions related to real estate that involve securities will require compliance with the Oregon Securities Law. These include the following:

- Selling a mortgage or other real estate financing instrument containing a promise to pay in the future.

For Example	In order to get her property sold, an owner takes back a purchase money second mortgage for $10,000. The seller needs cash; the real estate broker agrees to help find someone to buy the real estate paper from her. He finds two investors, each willing to invest $5,000. When he arranges the sale of the second mortgage to them, he has engaged in a securities transaction.

- Selling an incorporated business when the transaction involves the transfer of the common stock of that business.

For Example	After a ranch in Eastern Oregon was listed by the owner, the listing broker found a purchaser. However, the ranch was incorporated, and the owner was actually the owner of all common stock of the corporation. The sale actually involved the transfer of ownership of the common stock in the corporation (the corporation is the owner of the real estate), rather than the transfer of the real property itself.

- Offering a security as an inducement to purchase real property or to enter into other types of real estate transactions.
- Selling limited partnership interests.

For Example	A local investor owns a limited partnership interest in an investment group, often called a *syndicate*, which is buying property and developing a shopping center. The businessperson owning that interest contracts with a broker to help her sell her interest.

- Offering, as an investment contract, participation in real estate paper; or an interest in a pool of trust deeds, mortgages, or land sale contracts, such as when the owner of one interest in a pool of trust deeds asks a broker to help sell that interest.
- Selling condominium securities. The offering of condominium units would be considered an offering of securities in the form of investment contracts if the offering is coupled with any of the following:

- The offering of participation in a rental pool arrangement. A rental pool is a device whereby a promoter or a third party agrees to rent the condo unit on behalf of the owner at times the unit is not being used by the owner. Income and expenses involved in renting all the units in the condo are combined. Each owner then receives a share of the profits, regardless of which units were actually rented.

For Example	A 100-unit hotel was taken over by new owners who convert it into a condominium. Individual units are sold as investments with the contract authorizing management by individuals other than those owning units and spelling out details of distribution of income. The offer involves an offering of an investment contract, since a purchaser would expect financial benefit in the form of appreciation, tax shelter and/or cash flow and the units would be managed by the promoter or an independent third party.

  - An offering of a rental or similar arrangement whereby the purchaser must hold his unit available for rental for any part of the year, use an exclusive renting agent, or be otherwise materially restricted in the occupancy or rental of his unit.
  - An offering of a rental arrangement or other similar service emphasizing the benefits to the purchaser resulting from the efforts of the promoter or a third party in connection with the rental of the units.

In addition, the following activities may or may not be subject to the securities law, depending on the circumstances of the individual transaction:
- Selling interests in a general partnership, joint venture, cooperative or unincorporated association formed for the purpose of investment in real property
- A sale-leaseback, wherein an owner sells his property to an investor and, at the same time, leases back the property
- Selling franchises
- Selling timeshare estates that are exempt from regulation by the Agency

An exemption of significance to real estate licensees applies to the sale of a whole note with a mortgage or trust deed, or of a seller's entire interest in a land sales contract to one purchaser in one transaction. However, the licensee may need to be licensed as a mortgage broker.

Under state law, unless a specific exemption applies, a security may not be offered or sold until it is registered with the Director of the Department of Consumer and Business Services. Securities may only be offered or sold through a person licensed by the appropriate federal and state agencies, *unless* there is a specific exemption to the licensing requirement. In any offer or sale of securities, there must be full, accurate, and complete disclosure of all material facts, even if there is an exemption from registration or licensing.

The offering of Oregon securities to non-Oregon residents and non-Oregon securities to Oregon residents must comply with registration and prospectus delivery requirements of the Federal Securities Act and must comply with the anti-fraud provisions of the Securities Exchange Act.

Brain Teaser

Reinforce your understanding of the material by correctly completing the following sentences:

1. Rules to implement the law are created by the _____ _____ _____.

2. A broker is not permitted to engage in professional real estate activity independently of a _____ _____ supervision and control.

3. The state agency that issues real estate licenses and enforces the provisions of the Real Estate License Law is called the _____ _____ _____.

Brain Teaser Answers

1. Rules to implement the law are created by the **Real Estate Commissioner**.

2. A broker is not permitted to engage in professional real estate activity independently of a **principal broker's** supervision and control.

3. The state agency that issues real estate licenses and enforces the provisions of the Real Estate License Law is called the **Real Estate Agency**.

Review – Oregon Licensing

This lesson explores the requirements for holding a real estate license in Oregon, and the roles of the Real Estate Agency, Real Estate Commissioner and Real Estate Board.

License Required

The Oregon Real Estate License Law is contained in Chapter 696. Rules to implement the law are created by the Real Estate Commissioner and are contained in Oregon Administrative Rules Section 863.

To perform professional real estate activity for another and for compensation a person must be licensed. A person with a real estate broker license is authorized to engage in all professional real estate activity, as a broker associated with a principal real estate broker. A principal broker is authorized to employ, engage or otherwise supervise other real estate licensees. A real estate property manager licensee may only engage in the management of rental real estate.

ORS 696 does not apply to a general partner for a limited partnership while engaging in the sale of limited partnership interests and while engaging in the acquisition, sale, exchange, lease, transfer or management of the real estate of the limited partnership; a person performing an act of professional real estate activity under order of a court; persons whose business or jobs are real estate related but are not of the same nature as real estate brokerage, such as a financial institution or trust company acting as an attorney-in-fact or a salaried government employee; a person selling or leasing cemetery lots, selling membership camping contracts, and those who arrange rental of transient lodging at hotels and inns; certain professionals when performing services in performance of their professions, including an attorney at law, registered professional engineer or architect, and professional forester or farm manager.

Those exempt from the need for a real estate license to perform various real estate activities under specified conditions, but subject to provisions of the license law and administrative rules and regulations in performing real estate transactions if they do hold a real estate license, include a consultant who analyzes or advises permissible land use alternatives, environmental impact, building and use permit procedures, or demographic market studies; a paid fiduciary whose real estate activity is limited to negotiating or closing a transaction to obtain the services of a real estate licensee; person acting as a fiduciary under a court order; a person engaging in real estate transactions for himself; a persons acting as an attorney-in-fact under a power of attorney; a nonlicensed regular full-time employee of a single owner of real estate if his real estate activity is not his principal activity, or if his real estate activity is his principal activity, but his employer's principal activity or business is not the sale, exchange, lease option or acquisition of real estate; a nonlicensed regular full time employee of a single owner in the rental or management of real property; and a nonlicensed individual employed by a real estate broker, principal real estate broker, or property manager and acting as a manager for real estate if his real estate activity is limited to negotiating rental or lease agreements, checking tenant and credit references, physically maintaining the real estate, conducting tenant relations, collecting the rent, supervising the premises managers (i.e., resident managers), and discussing financial matters relating to management of the real estate with the owner.

Real Estate Agency and Commissioner

The state agency that issues real estate licenses and enforces the provisions of the Real Estate License Law is called the Real Estate Agency (the Agency). The Agency is under the supervision and control of an administrator, the Real Estate Commissioner (the Commissioner). A Real Estate Board is established within the Agency as an advisory board. Neither the Agency nor the Board is set up to handle disputes between licensees.

License Qualifications

To qualify for any real estate license, an applicant must have a high school diploma, GED or international equivalent, be at least 18 years of age, submit a license application and fees, complete the required education, pass any required exam, and submit a background check application and fingerprints to show he is trustworthy and competent. He need not be a resident or a citizen of Oregon. A broker applicant must designate the principal real estate broker with whom he will be associated if he intends to have an active license.

To qualify for a principal real estate broker license, an applicant must pass a 48-question principal broker exam, have three years of active experience and furnish proof of successful completion of an Agency-approved 40-hour course in brokerage administration and sales supervision.

To qualify for a real estate property manager license, an applicant must submit his license application and fee, provide fingerprints, successfully complete a 60-hour property management course and pass a 100-question real estate property manager license examination, indicate the name under which he will operate or identify the property manager or principal broker with whom he will be associated.

All licenses are issued for a term expiring at the end of the licensee's birth month the second year after issuance. To qualify an active license for renewal, the licensee must present evidence of attendance at 30 clock-hours of real estate-related continuing education courses in required course topics. A 30-hour advanced real estate practices course must be completed by a broker licensee prior to his first renewal of an active license.

Transactions related to real estate that involve securities will require compliance with the Oregon Securities Law.

Oregon Listing and Disclosure

Overview

This lesson discusses restrictions on activities of a licensee related to the listing of a property. Such activities include preparing a competitive market analysis, offering the property for sale, listing and advertising the property and providing disclosures of the property condition.

Objectives

Upon completion of this lesson, the student should be able to:

1. Explain when a licensee may perform a competitive market analysis and what must be included in it.
2. Describe the authorization necessary to offer property for sale and place For Sale signs on property.
3. Describe requirements and prohibitions regarding listings.
4. Describe the requirements and restrictions that apply to advertising by a licensee, including the principal broker's role in supervising such advertising.
5. Explain what types of facts are material or not material in relation to disclosure requirements.
6. Discuss property condition disclosure requirements imposed on sellers by the state statutes.

Listings

A successful listing of property will include preparing a competitive market analysis that will provide the owner with the data to enable him to properly price his property for sale in the current market, preparing a listing agreement in compliance with all regulatory requirements and ensuring that all necessary disclosures about the title and property are made.

----- COMPETITIVE MARKET ANALYSIS -----

License to Appraise

The **Appraiser Certification and Licensure Board (ACLB)** of the Department of Consumer and Business Services administers the appraiser license program. The appraiser licensing law defines real estate **appraisal activity** as the preparation, completion and issuance of an opinion as to the value on a given date or at a given time of real property or any interest in real property, whether or not such activity is performed in connection with a federally related transaction. A federally related transaction is real estate-related financial transaction involving a federal agency or financial institution regulated or insured by a federal agency.

The appraiser licensing law provides that no person may engage in or carry on real estate appraisal activity within this state without first obtaining certification or licensure. It also provides that a state-certified appraiser or a state-licensed appraiser is not required to have a real estate license to perform any real estate appraisal activity or any other activity that constitutes the giving of an opinion as to the value of real property or any interest in real property. As such, a state-certified or state-licensed appraiser is not subject to regulation under the real estate license law.

Real Estate Licensee Exemption

A real estate broker is not able to appraise unless he obtains a separate appraiser license from the ACLB, but he is exempt from appraisal licensing for the following activities:

- If compelled to give an opinion in a judicial or administrative proceeding by judicial order or subpoena
- If giving an opinion regarding the value of real estate for taxation
- If analyzing an interest in real estate for purposes of a lending collateral analysis or a default collateral analysis, when the analysis is used only for internal purposes of a lending institution and, in the case of a lending collateral analysis, the loan transaction at issue is valued at less than $250,000. A **lending collateral analysis** is a real property market analysis prepared for use by a lending institution in support of a loan application. A **default collateral analysis** is a real property market analysis for use by a lending institution in considering its options with respect to a loan in default. If a licensee completes a lending collateral analysis or default collateral analysis on a property in which he has either a current, active listing agreement or is representing the buyer or seller in a pending transaction on the property, he must disclose to the buyer and seller his relationship with the lending institution.

Real estate licensees are also exempted from appraisal licensing if giving a competitive market analysis (CMA) or letter opinion as defined in the real estate licensing law. The real estate licensing law provides that a principal broker or broker may give letter opinions or perform competitive market analyses for listing and offer purposes, by including in its definition of professional real estate activity, the offer, attempt or agreement:

- to perform or provide a competitive market analysis or letter opinion;
- to represent a taxpayer before a Tax Court magistrate or the Department of Revenue in any conference or proceeding with respect to the administration of any ad valorem property tax, or by signing and verifying a petition to the board of property tax appeals on behalf of the taxpayer; or
- to give an opinion in any administrative or judicial proceeding regarding the value of real estate for taxation.

CMA and Letter Opinion

The objective of a CMA or letter opinion is to help formulate a recommended listing, selling or purchase price, or rental or lease consideration.

The law defines a **competitive market analysis** as "a method or process used by a real estate licensee in pursuing a listing agreement or in formulating an offer to acquire real estate in a transaction for the sale, lease, lease-option or exchange of real estate." Its objective is a recommended listing, selling or purchase price or a lease or rental consideration. It may be expressed as an opinion of the value of the real estate in a contemplated transaction. It may include, but is not limited to, an analysis of market conditions, public records, past transactions and current listings of real estate.

A **letter opinion** (often referred to as a broker price opinion, or BPO) is defined as a document that expresses a real estate licensee's conclusion regarding a recommended listing, selling or purchase price or a rental or lease consideration of certain real estate that results from the licensee's competitive market analysis. A letter opinion not based on a CMA would be in violation of the license law requirements.

Real estate licensees can express their findings in a CMA in terms of the value of property and use the term "value" or similar terms when they are compelled to do so.

For Example	Andy Bellum, a real estate licensee, was hired to conduct a competitive market analysis and issue a written letter opinion on a recommended listing/selling price for a property. In court, the judge asked Andy whether he believed the recommended listing price to be the value of the property in question. Andy was allowed to express an opinion of value without fear of sanction by the ACLB.

The term **value** as used in a competitive market analysis or letter opinion is the estimated worth of or price for a specific property. It is not intended to mean or imply the value was arrived at by any method of appraisal. Therefore, this value is not the appraised value of the property.

Although a real estate licensee may offer a CMA for the purpose of establishing a listing or selling price, or give a letter opinion, he must be careful not to let the recipient of the analysis or opinion believe that it is an opinion of the appraised value of the real estate.

Oregon license law and administrative rules have a few specific requirements regarding CMAs and letter opinions.

- As with all other professional real estate activities, CMAs and letter opinions may be provided by a real estate broker only under the control and supervision of his principal broker.
- A real estate licensee can charge or accept compensation for a letter opinion, a CMA or taxpayer representation, provided all fees received are paid through the principal broker to the licensee.
- A real estate licensee cannot accept employment or compensation for the preparation of a CMA or letter opinion that is contingent upon reporting a predetermined value or for real estate in which the licensee had an undisclosed interest. He cannot represent a taxpayer and receive compensation to prepare a CMA or letter opinion where his fee is contingent upon reporting a predetermined value.

The Commissioner's rules require that a CMA or letter opinion must be in writing and contain at least the following items:

- A statement of purpose and intent
- A brief description of the property
- The basis of reasoning used to reach the conclusion of value including the applicable market data and/or capitalization computation
- Any limiting conditions
- A disclosure of any existing or contemplated interest of the licensee in the subject property
- The signature of the licensee issuing the competitive market analysis or letter opinion and the date of its issuance
- A disclaimer that, unless the real estate licensee is also licensed by the ACLB, the report is not intended to meet the requirements set out in the Uniform Standards of Appraisal Practice
- A disclaimer that the CMA or letter opinion is not intended as an appraisal and that, if an appraisal is desired, the services of a competent professional licensed appraiser should be obtained

----- LISTINGS -----

A real estate licensee may advertise property only with the written permission of the owner or the owner's authorized agent.

He may offer real estate for sale or lease only with the knowledge and consent of the owner or the owner's authorized agent and only on terms authorized by the owner or the owner's authorized agent. He may place a sign on a property offering it for sale or for rent only with the written authority of the owner or the owner's authorized agent. The necessary consent to offer the property for sale, the terms of the sale, and the authority to place a For Sale sign on the property is typically provided in the listing agreement, signed by the owner or the owner's authorized agent. A licensee could have his license suspended or revoked if he were to display a For Sale sign on property without the written consent of the owner, quote a price other than the listing price stipulated by the owner, or act as the owner's agent prior to obtaining the listing for the property.

Agency regulations provide that every listing agreement, whether exclusive or nonexclusive:
- must state an expiration date. It does not need to show a beginning date, as the listing is effective once the broker has a signed copy in his possession.
- may not include any provision requiring the seller to notify the broker of the seller's intention to cancel the listing after the stated, definite expiration date.
- may not contain any provision subjecting the seller of the listed property to the payment of two or more commissions for one sale if the seller lists the same property with a second or subsequent broker after the first or preceding listing agreement expires or is terminated by mutual agreement. Therefore, the safety (or protection) clause included in most exclusive listing agreements cannot be enforced if the owner immediately lists with another broker after the first listing expires.
- must be signed by all parties to the agreement.

If a buyer defaults in a transaction, the seller is entitled to the **forfeited earnest money** as liquidated damages. In Oregon, the question of the disposition of forfeited earnest money must be negotiated between the real estate broker and seller at the time of executing any listing agreement or earnest money agreement. The result of such negotiations could be any arrangement agreeable to the broker and the seller. It could provide for the seller to keep it all, the broker to keep it all up to the amount of his commission and the seller to get the rest, the broker to keep an amount equal to expenses and the seller to get the rest, or both to receive a percentage, (e.g., 50-50%, 25-75%, etc.). The result of the negotiation must be filled in on the agreement form at the time of signing by the seller and either separately initialed by the seller or placed immediately above the signature of the seller.

The Agency does not require that the listing:
- be on an approved form.
- be an exclusive listing.
- have an effective date.
- require the seller to allow the broker to distribute the listing through a multiple listing service.
- be acknowledged (as listings are not recorded).

A licensee must, at the time of securing the listing, give the person signing, the owner or his authorized agent, a true legible copy of the listing. The licensee does not give a copy to the buyer or the prospective buyer. In addition, the licensee must give a copy to his principal broker, as the listing belongs to the principal broker. This copy must be reviewed by the principal broker or branch manager within seven business days of the day the listing was accepted. It is then kept in the principal broker's office as part of his transaction records. If the listing licensee transfers his license to another principal broker, his listing remains with the original principal broker until it is terminated.

A licensee cannot alone or with other persons enter into activity to deprive the original listing broker of a commission or intentionally interfere with the exclusive representation or exclusive brokerage relationship of another licensee. When a licensee knows an owner, purchaser or lessor has a written outstanding contract for exclusive representation by another principal broker in negotiations in connection with a property, the licensee may deal directly with that owner, purchaser or lessor only with the prior written consent of the other licensee.

----- ADVERTISING -----

In the Commissioner's rules, **advertising** includes all forms of representation, promotion and solicitation disseminated in any manner and by any means of communication for any purpose related to professional real estate activity. This means it includes, without limitation, advertising by:

- mail.
- telephone, cellular telephone, and telephonic advertising
- the Internet, E-mail, electronic bulletin board and other similar electronic systems.
- business cards.
- signs, lawn signs, and billboards.

Name
The licensed name or registered business name of the principal broker or property manager must be prominently displayed, immediately noticeable, and conspicuous in all advertising.

For Example	If Matthew Donaldson, an Oregon broker, printed business cards for himself that read, "Matthew Donaldson, Licensed Real Estate Broker," Donaldson must also include in the ads or on the cards, the licensed name of the brokerage. The cards need not include any other details, e.g., Donaldson's home address, telephone number or real estate license number.

Advertising that includes the licensee's name must use:
- his licensed name; or
- a common derivative of his first name (e.g., Pat instead of Patricia) and his licensed last name.

A licensee's licensed name would include his surname with a combination of given names and initials. Business can be conducted with such a name either by itself or coupled with words describing the business.

Peter William Adams can operate as Peter William Adams, Peter W. Adams, Peter Adams, P.W. Adams, or any of these with such words as Realty, Real Estate, Realtor, Properties, Broker, etc.

A **business name** includes, but is not limited to, an assumed name or the name of a business entity such as a corporation, partnership, limited liability company, or other business entity recognized by law. If a business name includes words such as "Company," "and Company," or "and Associates" to suggest there are additional owners, the name becomes an assumed name requiring registration.

Oregon law requires that a name be registered with the Secretary of State when the business is conducted in a name that does not disclose the real and true name of each person carrying on, conducting or transacting the business. When the name the principal broker would use in business is such that it would constitute an assumed name, the Secretary of State must register it *before* it can be registered with the Real Estate Agency and a real estate license can be issued.

A principal broker may register two or more business names and conduct professional real estate activity separately under each business name if the business names are for affiliated or subsidiary business organizations.

The Agency's registration system for business names allows a principal broker to register the business name of a branch office. The principal broker operating under a registered business name need not be an owner or officer of any organization entitled to use the registered business name or have an ownership interest in the registered name. However, all professional real estate activity conducted by or on behalf of the principal broker must be conducted under that registered business name, as the registered business name has no license standing independent of the principal broker registering the business.

A broker associated with a principal broker is also required to conduct his activities in his full licensed name. Often a licensee is known in his marketing area by some name other than his given name. Under the license law, a person may use a nickname in the license only if the desired name is shown in parentheses in the license application.

Pete Adams could apply for a license as Peter (Pete) Adams, and his advertising and other professional real estate activity would be conducted using his full licensed name. Mary Smith, who just married Pete, could have her license as Mary (Smith) Adams. Their advertising and other professional real estate activity would be conducted using their full licensed name.

Contents

An advertisement offering listed property for sale need not include the seller's asking price, the location of the property, the date the property will be available for possession, or any other details.

Advertising by a licensee, in process and in substance, must:

- be truthful and not deceptive or misleading. It must be free from any misleading statements, including any misrepresentation as to the property itself, the terms of the sale, or the property value.
- not guarantee future profits from any real estate activity.
- be identifiable as advertising of a real estate licensee. It need not state that he is licensed, but must clearly give the impression that any property he is offering for sale is not being offered For Sale By Owner.
- not state or imply that he, if a broker or a property manager associated with a principal broker, is the person responsible for operating the real estate brokerage or is a principal broker.
- not state or imply that he is qualified or has a level of expertise other than that he currently maintains.
- be done only with the written permission of the property owners or their authorized agent. A licensee may only advertise, display and distribute information about properties, whether or not listed for sale, lease, or exchange with him or with his principal broker, if he has first obtained written permission of the owner or the owner's authorized agent.

Principal Broker Responsibility

A principal broker must review all advertising of a broker or a property manager who is associated with him and is responsible for all advertising approved by him that states his licensed name or registered business name. However, he may delegate direct supervisory authority and responsibility for advertising originating in a branch office to the principal broker who manages the branch office, if he does so in writing.

A licensee associated with a principal broker may advertise his own property for sale, exchange, or lease option without the principal broker's approval, if:

- the property is not listed for sale, exchange, or lease option with the principal broker.
- the advertising states that the property owner is a real estate licensee.
- the advertising complies with all other applicable provisions of the license law and its implementing rules.

Electronic Media

Advertising in electronic media and by electronic communication (e.g., the Internet, web pages, E-mail, E-mail discussion groups, blogs, and bulletin boards) by a licensee must include on its first page:

- a statement that he is licensed in Oregon.
- his licensed name.
- the licensed name or registered business name of the principal broker or property manager.

However, exempt from these requirements are:

- sponsored links (i.e., paid advertisements located on a search engine results page), if the first page following the link complies with the requirement.
- E-mail from a licensee, if his initial communication contained the required information.

In addition, all advertising in electronic media and by electronic communication must comply with all other requirements of the advertising rule.

Team Advertising

A licensee may use the term "team" or "group" to advertise only if:

- the team or group includes at least one real estate licensee.
- all licensee members are associated with the same principal broker or property manager.
- each licensee member uses his licensed name as required.
- if any non-licensed individuals are named in the advertising, the advertising must clearly state which individuals are licensees and which ones are not.
- the use of the term does not constitute the unlawful use of a trade name and is not deceptively similar to a name under which any other person is lawfully doing business.
- the advertising complies with all other applicable provisions of the license law and its implementing rules.

Disclosures

Material Facts

Real estate licensees and property owners have a duty to disclose material facts to prospective property buyers.

However, under state law certain facts that do not adversely affect the physical condition of or title to the property are not included in the category of material facts and need not be disclosed. Among those incidents that are not material facts to a real property transaction and, therefore, need not be disclosed by a seller or a real estate agent in a transaction are the following:

- The fact or suspicion that the real property or a neighboring property was the site of a death by violent crime, by suicide or by any other manner
- The fact or suspicion that a convicted registered sex offender (registered under ORS 181.595, 181.596 or 181.597) resides in the area (In addition, the real estate license law specifically provides that nothing in the statutes relating to registration of sex offenders or licensing of real estate agents creates an obligation on the part of a real estate licensee to disclose to a potential purchaser of residential property that a registered convicted sex offender resides in the area.)
- The fact or suspicion that the real property or a neighboring property was the site of a crime, political activity, religious activity or any other act or occurrence that does not adversely affect the physical condition of or title to real property
- The fact or suspicion that an owner or occupant of the real property has or had human immunodeficiency virus (HIV) or acquired immune deficiency syndrome (AIDS)

Seller's Property Condition Disclosure

Most sellers of residential property in Oregon are required to complete a Seller Property Disclosure form and deliver it to the purchaser unless the seller is exempt. The language in the form is statutory which means it can't be changed and the language is set out in ORS 105.464. The form covers things such as conditions of the title, the condition of the roof and other systems in the home such as plumbing, electrical, and water, septic and sewer systems. A copy of the form can be found online at:
https://olis.leg.state.or.us/liz/2013R1/Downloads/MeasureDocument/HB3299/Introduced

Unless the seller qualifies for an exemption the completed form must be delivered to the buyer. After the seller has delivered the completed form to the buyer, the buyer has five days to revoke their offer. If the seller fails to comply, the buyer is entitled to revoke their offer to purchase any time prior to closing the sale.

Licensees should be careful not to fill out the form for a seller or influence their answers under any circumstances. And, if a licensee is aware that a seller improperly answered a question, the licensee is under an obligation to disclose that fact to a buyer or buyer's agent if the answer relates to a material defect. Sellers should be reminded that just filling

out the form does not relieve the seller of the duty to disclose any other material defects that may not be a subject of a question on the form.

Property Subject to the Law
The disclosure law applies only to residential real estate that consists of or is improved by one to four dwelling units, such as a single-family home, a duplex, a triplex or a four-plex, but not to any property larger than a four-plex. A manufactured structure would be considered a residential dwelling unit subject to the disclosure requirements when the structure and its site are owned by the same owner, have been assessed for property tax purposes as real property, and are being sold as one unit. On the other hand, a manufactured dwelling on leased land (such as in a mobile home park) is considered personal property and not subject to the disclosure requirements. Also, all nonresidential real estate is exempt.

The disclosure law does not apply to a leasehold, but it does apply to a lease-option of the specified residential property.

In the following situations, this law does not apply, because other laws require the seller to provide a different disclosure to the buyer:
- The sale of a lot in a planned community when a Statement of Planned Community Information is required. It does apply when the statement is not required.
- The first sale of new condominium units where the Oregon Condominium Act requires the developer or his agent to give a disclosure statement to the first buyer of a condominium unit for residential use. The law does apply to resales of previously occupied condominium units.
- Timeshare properties, when the timeshare laws require the developer or the developer's agent to provide a copy of a public report for the timeshare plan. Because only timeshare developments of 13 or more units are subject to the timeshare public report requirements, small timeshare developments consisting of 12 or fewer units are subject to the property condition disclosure requirements.

Transactions Not Subject to the Law
For those sellers who cannot be expected to have knowledge of the property condition because they either have never resided in the property or are unfamiliar with the property, the law exempts the following transactions:
- Sales or transfers by governmental agencies
- Sales by financial institutions that acquired the property as custodian, agent or trustee, or by foreclosure or deed in lieu of foreclosure
- Sales by court-appointed receivers, personal representatives of estates, trustees, conservators or guardians (The law would apply and disclosure would be required for  sales ordered by a court where the court did not appoint a third party to sell the property. For example, if a court orders a couple to sell their property and split the proceeds as part of a divorce settlement, the sale would be subject to the provisions of the disclosure law, since the sellers were not acting as officers of the court.)

- The first sale of a dwelling never occupied, i.e., the sale of a new home, so long as the seller gives the buyer a brief disclosure that includes the permit number(s) under which the home was built and inspected and the name of the jurisdiction that issued the permit(s) (This information allows the buyer to check with the permit issuer and see whether there were any problems in the construction of the dwelling. To qualify for the exemption, the seller must provide the buyer with the following statement on or before the date the buyer is legally obligated to purchase the subject real property: "THIS HOME WAS CONSTRUCTED OR INSTALLED UNDER BUILDING OR INSTALLATION PERMIT(S) # ___ ISSUED BY ____." A seller of new construction who failed to provide this exact permit statement by the time he and the buyer have signed the purchase agreement would have to give a disclosure and allow the buyer a right of revocation. If the seller failed to give a disclosure at all, the buyer would have a right to revoke the transaction and receive a refund of his earnest money up until closing, even if the home was already under construction.)

Disclosure Statement

A property condition disclosure statement must be in substantially the form set forth in the statute. This form represents a statement of the seller's response to specific questions relating to the known condition of the most common concerns in residential real estate. A licensee representing the seller should urge the seller to be complete in his answers to the questions as the disclosures are required by law. The seller should not leave a space blank and should provide explanations where appropriate. If a question does not fit the seller's property, clarification should be provided. If an existing condition of the property exists but is not covered by the questions, that condition should be addressed in the question asking whether the seller is aware of any other material defects affecting the property or its value that a prospective buyer should know about.

The questions ask for the seller's knowledge of certain facts about the property; they do not ask whether the conditions exist. The disclosure form is not a warranty of the condition of the property, guaranteeing the future condition of the property. However, each of the disclosures is a material representation and, therefore, must be truthful as to the seller's knowledge.

Because the law also applies to property in which the seller does not live, the seller must disclose whether he is or is not occupying the property. This is because a disclosure of the condition based on the knowledge of a person not living in the property would be less of an accurate reflection of the property's condition than one completed by the current resident on the property, and the buyer should be made aware of the probable limited knowledge of the seller.

When signing the disclosure form, the seller attests to the truth of his disclosures. When there are two or more sellers of a property, the form provides spaces for each seller's signature. In some situations, such as divorce, all of the sellers may not have the same knowledge about the condition of the property and may prefer to fill out and sign separate disclosure statements.

In the form, the buyer is advised to obtain and pay for the services of a qualified specialist to inspect the property on his behalf (e.g., an architect, engineer, plumber, electrician, roofer, building inspector, or pest and dry rot inspector) in order to obtain a more comprehensive examination of the specific condition of the property. In signing the form, the buyer acknowledges his duty to pay diligent attention to any material defects that are known to him or can be known by him through diligent attention and observation. Therefore, the buyer cannot act irresponsibly by ignoring obvious material defects not disclosed by the seller or by unreasonably relying upon a questionable disclosure by the seller.

The buyer is advised that, unless he waives his right of revocation, he has five business days after the seller's delivery of the disclosure to revoke his offer by disapproving the seller's disclosure.

It is seller's duty to provide the property condition disclosure statement upon acceptance of the buyer's offer, even if the buyer obtained a completed form earlier. The seller has the burden of proof as to delivery of the disclosure statement or any amendment to the buyer who signed the sales agreement.

Buyer's Rights

The property condition disclosure law gives the buyer the right to waive his right to revoke at or before entering into a sales agreement. A buyer might waive his right because the seller insists that he will not accept an offer if the buyer does not do so, or to obtain more favorable consideration when there are competing offers.

If the buyer does waive his rights, his agent should obtain signed written documentation that he explained the buyer's revocation rights and the buyer, understanding those rights, decided to waive them. He should notify the seller about the waiver, retain the signed waiver in his transaction file, and give a copy of it to the broker or escrow agent closing the transaction.

A buyer who does not waive his right of revocation has five business days after delivery of the seller's disclosure statement to revoke the offer. Since the revocation period begins after delivery, the buyer (a term which includes all persons signing the "buyer's acceptance" portion of the disclosure statement) is required to acknowledge receipt of the disclosure statement (including any attachments) bearing the seller's signature. If a buyer or his agent refuses to accept a disclosure offered directly by the seller or through the seller's agent, the attempted delivery and refusal should be documented in a written note or memo giving the time, date and circumstances.

A buyer may revoke his offer within the allotted revocation period by delivering to the seller a separate signed written statement stating he disapproves the seller's disclosure and wishes to revoke his offer.

If the seller fails or refuses to provide a disclosure as required, the buyer has a right of revocation until the closing of the transaction. **Closing** means the point in the transaction where the buyer has signed all necessary final closing instructions and has executed all documents needed to conclude the transaction. Once the buyer closes the transaction, his right to revoke based on the property condition disclosure law is terminated. His right of revocation does not extend beyond closing of the transaction. A buyer who does revoke the offer under the rights provided by this law is entitled to the immediate return of all deposits and other considerations delivered to any party or escrow agent with respect to his offer and his offer is void. Upon receipt of the buyer's written request for the return of the funds, the escrow agent or broker holding the earnest money must return it to the buyer, without asking the seller for his consent. However, they may require the buyer to give written release and indemnification before returning the funds to him, so they will be released from all liability for those funds.

If the funds were deposited as a check or other noncash bank item, the broker or escrow agent must wait until funds have been placed in the broker's or escrow agent's clients' trust account. If the buyer has signed an earnest money promissory note, the broker or escrow agent must return it. The broker or escrow agent should keep proof of the return to show compliance with the law.

Licensee Duties

The requirements of the real estate disclosure law in Oregon apply to all sellers of real estate subject to the law. It applies to property that is listed with a real estate licensee or sold directly to a buyer by the seller in a "For Sale By Owner" format. The only affirmative duty placed on a licensee by the law is to advise his client of their rights and obligations under the disclosure law.

A real estate licensee representing the seller would be required to advise the seller of his duties to deliver a disclosure statement at the time of taking the listing, even if only to claim an exemption from the law.

A real estate licensee representing the buyer would be required to advise the buyer of his right to receive a disclosure, to revoke the offer within the appropriate time period, and to waive the right to revoke the offer. He should advise the buyer to carefully review the information provided to determine if it is complete and contains any explanations that are called for. He should also advise the buyer to have the property professionally inspected, regardless of whether he received a disclosure, provide the inspector with a copy of the information provided by the seller, and be present as the property is inspected, to see and discuss items noted by the inspector.

A real estate licensee has no affirmative duty to advise an unrepresented party in the transaction of their rights or duties under this law. However, he is not prohibited from doing so, and it is possible that failure to advise the unrepresented party could be considered a violation of his duty to act honestly and in good faith. Therefore, many licensees will provide a general description of the disclosure laws covering both the seller's obligations and the buyer's rights as a means of answering the questions of both buyer and seller.

The obligation to disclose defects rests with the seller, not any licensee. A real estate agent has no duty to inspect listed property, to find and report material defects. However, he cannot conceal material defects discovered on the property, even if disclosed in confidence by the seller, and is liable for negligent misrepresentation of defects that he should have recognized because of his specialized real estate knowledge and expertise.

Since all the questions on the form relate to the seller's knowledge of facts, a licensee should not fill out the disclosure statement for the seller and should not substitute his knowledge for the seller's knowledge of the information. If a licensee did fill out the form, he would have responsibility and liability for any mistakes or misrepresentations. A licensee may review the disclosure form with the seller to ensure that the seller has responded to all questions applying to the property. He may explain terms used and help interpret the meaning of questions asked in the form, but he should avoid telling the seller how to answer a question or advising the seller as to whether or not to disclose certain facts. He could, however, always advise full disclosure.

If a client is unsure of whether to disclose items that had been a problem in the past, but had since been repaired, disclosure would be the safest course of action. It would enable the buyer and/or his inspector to check to see if the repairs were adequate, and it may help in marketing the property by showing potential buyers that they were dealing with a seller who is not trying to hide anything.

When a seller makes obvious errors, innocent misrepresentations, or has omitted material facts which are discovered by the agent, his agent should question and discuss those obvious errors with the seller and urge the seller to amend the disclosure. A seller's agent cannot knowingly accept, without question, a disclosure statement that is clearly in error or out of date.

For Example

A seller may prepare a property condition disclosure which states that the roof does not leak. Two months later, after the rains have come, the ceiling shows water stains. The agent should, in such a case, challenge the seller by questioning the possible leak. The seller cannot dodge his responsibility to disclose material defects.

An agent, who knowingly fails to question an erroneous or out-of-date disclosure or does not strongly recommend that the seller amend or update it, creates potential civil liability for himself and the seller, as well as provides grounds for licensing sanctions by the Commissioner for misrepresentation by omission of a material fact. The seller's refusal to change the disclosure to more accurately reflect the condition of the property should be grounds for the agent to terminate the agency relationship.

Changes

A seller will often prepare the disclosure form at the time of listing the property. If a disclosed material condition changes after the disclosure statement has been prepared, the seller should make it known. If the seller advises his agent that there is a change in the information on the disclosure statement, the agent should make sure that the disclosure statement is amended or a new form is completed and make reasonable efforts to see that any existing copies of the outdated disclosure are changed or destroyed. Where there is an accepted offer from a buyer prior to the change, he should immediately disclose the changed information and get a signed receipt of acknowledgment from the buyer to place in the transaction file. Where the change is material to the transaction, it may affect the buyer's decision to go forward with the transaction. Issuance of an amendment would create a new disclosure statement and allow the buyer another five business days to rescind the contract.

Seller Refusal to Comply with the Law

If the seller refuses to provide a disclosure, his agent should make sure that the seller understands the requirements of the law and the effect of noncompliance. He should also obtain a written, signed statement from the seller that states that he has disclosed the seller's obligations to the seller. If the seller still refuses to disclose and because his agent cannot complete a disclosure for the seller, the agent should discuss with his principal broker whether they should withdraw from the agency relationship with the seller. If they do not terminate the agency relationship, they could be subject to common law actions as well as license law sanctions if material defects were not disclosed.

Real Estate Agency Requirements

All disclosures, and receipts for disclosures, delivered or received by the broker or his associates in the course of a real estate transaction must be reviewed and initialed by the principal broker in the same manner as are offers, counteroffers and other documents relating to the transaction and retained for six years.

Brain Teaser

Reinforce your understanding of the material by correctly completing the following sentences:

1. A _____ _____ transaction is real estate-related financial transaction involving a federal agency or financial institution regulated or insured by a federal agency

2. A real estate licensee may place a sign on a property offering it for sale or for rent only with the _____ _____ of the owner or the owner's authorized agent.

3. A licensee may only advertise properties if he has first obtained the written permission of the owner, or the owner's authorized _____.

4. The property condition disclosure law applies only to _____ real estate.

Brain Teaser Answers

1. A **federally related** transaction is real estate-related financial transaction involving a federal agency or financial institution regulated or insured by a federal agency.

2. A real estate licensee may place a sign on a property offering it for sale or for rent only with the **written authority** of the owner or the owner's authorized agent.

3. A licensee may only advertise properties if he has first obtained written permission of the owner or the owner's authorized **agent**.

4. The property condition disclosure law applies only to **residential** real estate.

Review — Oregon Listing and Disclosure

This lesson discusses restrictions on activities of a licensee related to the listing of a property.

Competitive Market Analysis

A real estate broker is exempt from appraisal licensing if compelled to give an opinion in a judicial or administrative proceeding by judicial order or subpoena; if giving an opinion regarding the value of real estate for taxation; if analyzing an interest in real estate for purposes of a lending collateral analysis or a default collateral analysis, when the analysis is used only for internal purposes of a lending institution and, in the case of a lending collateral analysis, the loan transaction at issue is valued at less than $250,000; or if giving a competitive market analysis (CMA) or letter opinion. The term "value" as used in a competitive market analysis or letter opinion is not the appraised value of the property.

CMAs and letter opinions may be provided only under the control and supervision of the principal broker. A real estate licensee can receive compensation, provided all fees are paid through the principal broker. He cannot receive employment or compensation for the preparation of a CMA or letter opinion that is contingent upon reporting a predetermined value or for real estate in which he had an undisclosed interest. He cannot represent a taxpayer contingent upon reporting a predetermined value.

Listing

A real estate licensee may advertise property only with the written permission of the owner or the owner's authorized agent. He may offer real estate for sale or lease only with the knowledge and consent of, and only on terms authorized by, the owner or the owner's authorized agent. He may place a For Sale or For Rent sign on a property only with the written authority of the owner or the owner's authorized agent.

Every listing agreement, whether exclusive or nonexclusive, must state a definite expiration date, may not include any provision requiring the seller to notify the broker of the seller's intention to cancel or not renew the listing after the stated, definite expiration date, and may not contain any provision subjecting the owner of the listed property to the payment of two or more commissions for one sale in the event the owner lists the same property with a second, or subsequent, broker after the termination of the first, or preceding, listing agreement.

Disposition of forfeited earnest money must be negotiated between the broker and seller at the time of executing any listing agreement or earnest money agreement. The result of the negotiation must be filled in on the agreement form at the time of signing by the seller and either separately initialed by the seller or placed immediately above the signature of the seller.

A licensee must, at the time of securing the listing, give the person signing, the owner or his authorized agent, a true legible copy of the listing. In addition, he must give a copy to his principal broker, as the listing belongs to the principal broker. This copy must be reviewed by the principal broker or branch manager within seven business days of the day the listing was accepted.

A licensee cannot alone or with other persons enter into activity to deprive the original listing broker of a commission or intentionally interfere with the exclusive representation or exclusive brokerage relationship of another licensee.

Advertising

In the Commissioner's rules, advertising includes all forms of representation, promotion and solicitation disseminated in any manner and by any means of communication for any purpose related to professional real estate activity, including the Internet, business cards, signs and telephonic greetings or answering machine messages.

All real estate advertising by a real estate licensee must be done in the principal broker's, sole principal broker's or property manager's licensed or registered business name. It must be truthful and not deceptive or misleading. A licensee may not use words that state or imply he is qualified or has a level of expertise other than that he actually has or imply that he is responsible for the operation of the brokerage, if he is associated with a principal broker; and his ad must be reasonably identifiable as advertising of a real estate licensee.

The principal broker is responsible for all real estate advertising of a licensee associated with him, except advertising of property owned by the licensee and not listed for sale or lease by the principal broker. Under written company policy, he may delegate direct supervisory authority over advertising originating in a branch office to the branch office manager. However, he remains responsible for all advertising done under his license.

Disclosures

Facts that do not adversely affect the physical condition of or title to a property do not fall into the category of material facts that must be disclosed. Oregon's property condition disclosure law requires that a seller provide a buyer of residential property with a completed disclosure form as part of the offer and the acceptance.

The disclosure law applies only to residential real estate that consists of or is improved by one to four dwelling units.

It is the seller's duty to provide a property condition disclosure statement upon acceptance of the buyer's offer. A buyer has the right to waive his right to revoke at or before entering into a sales agreement. A buyer who does not waive his right has five business days after delivery of the seller's disclosure statement to revoke the offer. If the seller fails or refuses to provide a disclosure as required, the buyer has a right of revocation until the closing of the transaction. A buyer who does revoke the offer under the rights provided by this law is entitled to the immediate return of all deposits and other considerations delivered to any party or escrow agent with respect to his offer, and his offer is void.

The only affirmative duty placed on a licensee by real estate agency law is to advise his client of their rights and obligations under the disclosure law. A real estate agent has no duty to inspect listed property to find and report material defects. However, he cannot conceal material defects discovered on the property, even if disclosed in confidence by the seller, and is liable for negligent misrepresentation of defects that he should have recognized because of his specialized real estate knowledge and expertise.

Oregon Sales

Overview

This lesson covers requirements relating to buying and selling real estate. Included are rules relating to writing and submitting offers and buying and selling property for oneself. Discussion of laws relating to fair housing concludes the lesson.

Objectives

Upon completion of this lesson, the student should be able to:

1. Describe the duties of a licensee in writing and presenting an offer or counteroffer.
2. Identify the required contents of an offer.
3. Explain the functions and license requirements of participants in a real estate auction.
4. Recite the most significant legal requirements, from the standpoint of a licensee, for creation, initial sale and operation of timeshare plans.
5. Explain the different functions of the membership camping operator, contract salespersons, contract broker, and the real estate broker in marketing campground membership contracts.
6. Describe how a licensee's own purchases and sales of real estate are regulated by the license law.
7. Describe how the license law relates to a licensee's management of his own property.
8. Describe the fair housing protections offered under state law.

Sales Offers and Counteroffers

----- OFFERS -----

An offer, such as an earnest money agreement, signed by a prospective buyer is an offer to purchase, regardless of any pending inspections, conditions or other contingencies. A real estate licensee is not required to write an offer to purchase on any particular form. It need not be on a form approved, or even reviewed, by the Agency. The Agency, unlike other real estate licensing entities elsewhere, does not design the form, mandate the use of a particular form, or pass judgment on forms used by licensees, unless there is a complaint filed against a licensee.

Contents

Administrative rules require that, when writing an offer to purchase, a licensee must include all of the terms and conditions of the real estate transaction in the offer. When writing a counteroffer, the licensee must include, directly or indirectly, all the terms and conditions of the transaction, in the counteroffer.

The terms and conditions in the earnest money agreement must include three specific items:
1. Whether the transaction will be accomplished by way of deed or land sales contract
2. Whether and at what time evidence of title (i.e., title insurance) is to be furnished to the prospective buyer
3. The type of earnest money received in the real estate transaction, whether in the form of cash, check or promissory note, personal property, etc.

> **For Example**
>
> A broker would be in violation of the Agency administrative rules if he obtained an offer to purchase with $10,000 earnest money but did not indicate in the offer the type of earnest money received from the purchaser.

The administrative rules do not favor or prohibit any form of earnest money. Therefore, earnest money in the form of personal property or a personal note would be acceptable.

> **For Example**
>
> A broker obtained an earnest money offer from a buyer who had no cash and therefore made his earnest money deposit in the form of a personal note for $4,000, payable in 10 days from the date of acceptance of the offer. The broker is permitted to accept such a personal note as an earnest money deposit, if he advises the seller of this prior to the seller's acceptance of the offer.

In order to ensure that the seller has legal consideration for the acceptance of the offer, in preparing a promissory note for use as earnest money, a licensee must make the note payable:

- on acceptance of the offer by the seller; or
- within a stated time (e.g., five days) following the seller's acceptance.

Unless there is a written agreement to the contrary, the note must be made payable to the seller. If the broker does redeem the note, he may not take any money from the proceeds, as the money would be the client's funds held in trust for the seller.

If the earnest money is cash or a check, the offer will stipulate whether the broker will hold the earnest money in a clients' trust account or give it to an escrow agent to hold. If the offer provides that the broker is to hold the earnest money, it may stipulate that the earnest money is to be deposited into an interest-bearing account. If that is the case, it may specify that the interest will be given to the broker, to the seller, or to the buyer. Who would get the interest would be strictly up to the parties to the agreement.

A principal broker and his associates must use caution in writing up sales agreements, so as to avoid earnest money problems that could cause losses to the seller, the buyer or both. They can protect themselves against these problems by adhering to the following practices:

- Always select the sales agreement form designed for the type of transaction involved. If the form contains material and blank spaces that do not apply to the transaction, cross out the material, or at least write "N/A" in the blank spaces.
- Reduce all areas of the agreement in a transaction between the buyer and seller to writing.
- Carefully draft contingencies so they are detailed and clear enough that both parties are aware of their respective obligations so as to achieve the purpose of the party having the contingency drafted.
- Never draft an open-ended contingency; always specify a date for performance.
- Never use abbreviations as a shortcut; always clearly spell out the terms and conditions of the transaction.
- Make all disclosures in writing.
- Explain to both the buyer and seller the purpose of earnest money early in the process in order to avoid disputes later.
- Always use a separate document as an addendum to spell out details that do not fit on the sales agreement form.
- Always have all parties to the transaction date and sign or initial transaction documents, as required; never sign a transaction document for a buyer or seller without a recorded power of attorney.
- Pay careful attention to details and immediately involve the principal broker when any aspect of the transaction becomes unclear.

Since the principal broker must review the forms, he is liable for errors or omissions in them. He cannot avoid responsibility for the incompetence of his associated brokers. Therefore, it is important that the review of these documents be performed with care.

The following are some of the most common items to be considered, and when applicable, carefully written into a residential purchase agreement form (commercial, industrial, vacant land, farm or ranch, development and other type properties each impose additional or different knowledge requirements on the agent):

- Date and place the contract is signed by the buyer
- The full and correct name, address and identification of the buyer (The correct name of the buyer is a very important item. If the name of the buyer is misspelled or so poorly written that it cannot be deciphered, documents may be prepared incorrectly and have to be re-recorded, causing needless expense. The correct name of the seller should always appear either typed or printed someplace in the sales agreement, because his signature may be illegible. As most transactions are closed in escrow, the escrow closer needs to know how to contact the seller and purchaser. This means addresses, fax and phone numbers where the buyers and sellers may be reached must be legibly written in the agreement.)
- The form of the buyer's deposit, whether cash, check, promissory note, money order, or other, must be indicated. If a note is used, indicate when it is redeemable.
- Whether the selling broker, listing broker, escrow or other, will hold the earnest money
- Whether the deposit is to be held and not deposited until acceptance of the offer
- The purchase price of the property
- The terms of purchase, i.e., whether it is all cash, a new loan, loan assumption, taking title subject to an existing loan, seller carry back financing, etc. (The existing lender may have to be contacted to ensure he will not require that the loan be paid off upon sale.)
- The amount of time allowed for the seller to consider the buyer's offer, and to complete the transaction
- Whether any contingencies are clearly written to accomplish their intended purpose
- Whether the covenants, conditions, restrictions, easements, rights, or other conditions of record that affect the property are acceptable to the buyer
- Whether the deed to be executed by the seller will contain any unusual exceptions or reservations, and if so, whether the buyer approved of them
- Whether there are any stipulations or agreements with reference to any tenancies or rights of persons in possession of the property
- Whether the buyer has indicated a desire for property inspections
- Whether there are there any stipulations or agreements with reference to any facts a survey would reveal if made, such as the existence of a party wall, other encroachments, easements, etc.
- Whether there are any special or unusual costs or charges to be adjusted through the escrow
- Who will pay for the title policy, escrow services, and other customary charges
- If any special documents are to be drawn with regard to the transaction, who will prepare them

- If prorations are not to be made as of the date of the close of escrow, the date to be used
- If possession is to be given prior to, or after, the close of the escrow, the type of agreement to be prepared to cover this occupancy and who is to prepare it
- The names, addresses, and phone numbers of cooperating brokers
- Signatures of all parties to the contract
- If the buyer or seller is a licensee, disclosure of his license status and the fact that he is representing himself as the buyer or seller, whichever is applicable

Delivery

At the time a licensee obtains an offer to purchase real property or a counteroffer to the offer, he must give the individual signing, a true and legible copy of the offer or counteroffer. Therefore, if an offer, together with a cash deposit, is made on a parcel to the listing broker, a copy of the earnest money receipt stating the offer must be given to the prospective buyer immediately (i.e., as soon as he signs the offer, and before the seller has a chance to review the agreement).

Upon receipt of an offer signed by the buyer or a counteroffer signed by the seller, a licensee must promptly deliver it to the offeree or to the offeror for acceptance or rejection, regardless of whether the terms are reasonable or not and regardless of the status of any other offer. A licensee must deliver all written offers to purchase property promptly to the seller; but he need not inform a seller about oral offers to purchase.

If a licensee receives several offers on the same property at the same time, he must present each offer to the seller promptly upon receipt. He cannot hold any offers pending the seller's decision on any previous offers.

For Example	Broker Cindy Smith receives a full-price, cash-out offer on a listing which she holds. She presents the offer to the seller, who requests time to review the offer. Prior to the seller's acceptance of the offer, another offer from a cooperating principal real estate broker is received.
	Smith should promptly present the new offer to the seller. She cannot inform the cooperating principal broker that a full price offer has been received and presented to the seller and suggest that the offer be resubmitted if and when the first offer is rejected. She cannot hold the new offer until the seller decides on the first offer and then present the new offer to the seller. She cannot refuse to accept the new offer.

A licensee's license could be revoked or suspended if he failed to submit to an owner before his acceptance of an offer, all written offers received for property listed for sale. A licensee may not reject an offer without consulting the client.

For Example	On Wednesday, a seller indicated to his listing agent that he would not sell for anything less than the full price. Another agent then brought in an offer $3,000 below the listed price on Friday. The listing agent cannot refuse to present the offer promptly.

On the other hand, a licensee could accept an offer that would be binding on his client if he were given the proper authority, in the form of a power of attorney, by the client. However, this is not the common practice.

Therefore, in addition to any other obligation imposed by law or by the contract during the term of a listing agreement, a licensee must promptly deliver all written offers to purchase the listed property to the client, until the sale is final and escrow has closed.

Promptly means as soon as practical under the particular circumstances. In most cases, where one or both of the spouses work, a licensee would be expected to present an offer the evening of the same day it was received by the licensee, unless the offer is received  after the sellers would reasonably be expected to be in bed. When an offer is received during the day, it may be most practical for the agent to call the seller at work to arrange an appointment for that evening. If the seller is unavailable it may be most practical for the offer to be presented via electronic transmission.

If a seller, for family or religious reasons, does not wish to do business on a Saturday or Sunday, his wishes must be honored. If the licensee does not believe in doing business on such a day, it would be reasonable to not do so. However, he should inform the client of that fact at the time of listing the property.

To deliver an offer is to present it for acceptance. This does not mean the offer must be physically handed to the seller. A seller is free to accept or reject any offer, with as much or as little attention or consideration as he may wish to expend. If a licensee calls the seller and provides the seller with all of the information he wishes to have concerning the offer, the licensee has delivered the offer and complied with the rule requiring prompt delivery of the offer. If the seller tells the licensee he does not wish to visually see and analyze the offer, the licensee cannot force him to study it.

The seller may have any number of reasons for not having an interest in considering an offer:
- The offered price may be too low.
- The offer may involve seller financing.
- The closing date may not be suitable.
- The offer may be totally unreasonable, such as an offer where the buyer will receive cash back from the seller, or the buyer wants to make a "low ball" offer, or the offer is lower than an offer that has already been rejected.
- The seller may have already accepted an offer and does not wish to consider any others.

In these instances, the licensee would have no desire to make a trip to physically present the offer, and the seller would not want to be bothered with an obviously unacceptable offer. If the licensee did bring the offer to the seller, the seller may feel insulted by the offer or may simply get upset with the licensee for wasting the seller's time presenting an offer in person when he has been told the seller has no interest in the offer.

Iona Holme has accepted an earnest money agreement from Anita House. The pending sale has been noted in the MLS and posted on the sign in front of Iona's property. Iona is happy with the accepted offer and does not want to be bothered with any other offers. For whatever reason she gives, Iona has a right to reject the offer, sight unseen if she wishes. Iona is the party who makes the decision, not her broker. No matter how bad an offer may appear, a broker must promptly tender it to the seller.

If the seller does not actually review the written offer at the time of rejection, the licensee should guard against the possibility of a claim by the seller that he had not been made aware of a written offer or a claim by another licensee that an offer had not been tendered. He may do this by following up a phone conversation with an electronic transmission of the offer or mailing a photocopy to the seller. He could ask the seller to mark the copy as "rejected," initial it and then send a copy back, or simply include a short cover letter describing the conversation and reminding the seller of the rejection.

"Based on our conversation on _____, we have informed _____ that their offer has been rejected. Enclosed is a copy of the rejected offer for your records."

It is important to ensure that each party receives a completed copy of the agreement within a reasonable time after both parties have signed it. After presenting an offer to the seller, a licensee must provide the seller with a true copy of the offer, whether the offer is accepted, countered or rejected.

If the seller or buyer rejects an offer or counteroffer, the licensee must provide a true copy to the party who made the offer or counteroffer. This copy may have the seller's initialed or signed rejection on it or a note by the licensee of the seller's rejection on it.

If the licensee obtains a written acceptance of an offer or a counteroffer, he must deliver within three banking days true, legible copies, signed by the seller and the purchaser, to both the seller and the purchaser.

The buyer will want a copy of the contract signed by the seller to compare to the copy he originally signed when making the offer. Also, the licensee will want to have the buyer sign and date the contract to acknowledge the seller's signature. The buyer's signature is not needed to make the contract binding, but it does provide proof that the buyer was notified of the seller's acceptance, and the buyer can withdraw his offer until he has been notified of the seller's signed acceptance of the offer.

As a result, a number of copies of the agreement are needed:

- The licensee is required to give two copies to the purchaser. The first he must give as soon as the prospective buyer signs the offer. The second he must give as soon as the offer is accepted or rejected by the seller.
- The licensee is required to give the seller one copy as soon as he signs the offer.
- A copy must be reviewed, initialed, and dated by the branch manager or principal broker within seven business days after is it accepted, rejected or withdrawn, and then maintained in the broker's office. A written record of the date and time of the delivery of each offer or counteroffer must be maintained in the offer or transaction file, along with a written record of the offeree's response to the offer.
- If the transaction is to be closed in escrow, an additional copy is needed for the escrow agent.

Once an offer has been accepted by the seller, a licensee no longer has a duty to seek additional offers. However, he does still have the duty to submit any offers received. A seller's agent has a duty to present all written offers, written notices and written communications to and from the parties in a transaction in a timely manner without regard to  whether the property is subject to a contract for sale or the buyer is already a party to a contract to purchase. Therefore, a licensee does not stop submitting offers just because the seller already has some under consideration or has even accepted one. He stops submitting them when the sale is final and escrow has closed.

For Example	When Broker Bea Real presented an offer to the seller, Iona Holme, Iona accepted the offer by signing and dating it. Bea then notified the buyer's agent that the offer had been accepted and the buyer's agent notified the buyer. The following day, Bea received another offer on the property from the agent of another buyer. Bea told the buyer's agent that the seller had already accepted an offer and therefore had a binding contract with another buyer. She refused to present the new offer to the seller. Bea has violated the law, as she was obligated to both the buyer and the seller to present all written offers.

----- AUCTIONS -----

A person who contracts through a listing or employment agreement to conduct a real estate auction must be a licensed principal broker. The principal broker conducting the auction is responsible for supervision of the auction and the activity of all licensed and unlicensed persons involved. He must make sure that those performing any acts of professional real estate activity (e.g., soliciting or negotiating) are appropriately licensed.

Bid assistants (often called spotters or ringmen) who merely spot bidders and clerks who do not become involved in professional real estate activity at the auction do not need to be licensed.

However, the auctioneer calling the auction must have a real estate license. In addition, any bid assistants who will answer questions about financing, payments, property condition or other matters while the auction is in progress, or "talk the sale up," by reminding bidders of the investment potential of the property or making other statements to induce them to bid higher must be licensed. These persons need to be licensed in order to ensure they are competent, knowledgeable and trustworthy, so as not to misrepresent the auctioned property or terms of sale.

When conducting a large auction, a principal broker may need additional licensees to answer questions and hold an open house for prospective bidders, who wish to inspect property prior to the auction, and may "co-op" the auction with another broker. The principal broker would enter into a written agreement listing the fees to be paid for the work performed. The principal broker would need to make sure that the licensees' association with their respective principal brokers are accurately represented as a licensee can only represent and conduct real estate activity in the name of the principal broker with whom he is associated.

Prior to conducting an auction, a broker should have a written listing agreement containing the terms, conditions and financing of the sale. These terms would be printed in the notice for the auction and in the bid package. They may include:
- whether owner financing is available.
- whether there will be reserve bids (bids made prior to the oral auction).
- whether the sale will be with reservation (a minimum price that must be met or exceeded before there is a sale).
- whether the sale will be absolute (without a sale reservation).
- the amount of any minimum starting bid.

The broker will normally collect an advance fee to cover the cost of advertising and setting up the auction.

Because the auction of real property must also comply with the requirements imposed by the license law and Agency regulations, auctioneers must provide complete disclosure of material defects in any property they auction, deposit earnest money in a trust account or in escrow, and have all agreements signed, reviewed and maintained for six years, just as they would for any other real estate transaction.

Auctions must comply not only with real estate license law, but with the Oregon Unlawful Trade Practices statute as well. Therefore, a complaint involving misrepresentation or fraud may be investigated by both the Agency and the State Attorney General. While the violation of license law could result in the loss of license, violation of the Unlawful Trade Practices statute could result in compensatory damages, punitive damages and attorney fees.

----- VACATION REAL ESTATE TIMESHARING -----

Since timeshare interests are considered real estate, persons involved in the sale of timeshares are subject to the real estate licensing laws and administrative rules. However, timeshare programs of 12 or fewer interests and timeshare programs for the shared use of personal property (e.g., motor homes, boats, airplanes) are not subject to timesharing and real estate licensing laws, although they are subject to other consumer protection laws, such as the property condition disclosure law.

A timeshare purchaser buys either ownership of a portion of the fee title to a vacation property or the right to use the property without fee ownership for a fixed period. Ownership or use is divided into time periods or timeshares. Each timeshare plan will spell out details of the ownership or use being offered.

The Timeshare Estates statutes set forth the legal requirements for creation, initial sale and operation of a timeshare plan. They require that:

- a public report prepared by the Agency to be given to purchasers prior to the signing of a binding contract.
- purchasers be given a five-calendar-day right of rescission to cancel a purchase without cause.
- holders of blanket encumbrances agree "not to disturb" the rights of purchasers to use the timeshare property upon a foreclosure of the encumbrance.
- timeshare developers reserve portions of money received from purchasers for the payment of blanket encumbrances to prevent foreclosure and ensure the availability of the timeshare property for timeshare purchasers.
- in the event of a failure of management to provide support services, scheduling and maintenance of accommodations and facilities, timeshare purchasers may, through their owners' association, replace the management to preserve their practical use of the timeshare program.

All individuals or real estate marketers who are engaged in direct contacts with Oregon prospects by phone or in person to procure their presence for a sales presentation must be licensed even if they are not physically located in Oregon. The marketing may be done by real estate licensees or through a separately licensed real estate marketing organization

(REMO). The REMO is licensed and supervised by one or more principal persons, who are screened by the Agency to make sure they are competent and trustworthy, and operates through employees registered with the Agency. These employees cannot sell the timeshares, but they may contact prospective purchasers to arrange visits to the development or to an off-site sales facility for the development, where a real estate licensee will engage in the actual sales activity with the prospective buyer.

While unlicensed timeshare owners cannot seek or accept referral fees or other compensation for referrals, they could be paid for referrals if, through a written agreement, they were actually employed and treated for tax purposes as employees of the REMO and were registered with the Agency as REMO employees.

A broker should not promote the availability of an exchange program as the main selling point of a sales presentation for a timeshare plan or promote a vacation timeshare for its investment potential, as most timeshares have not shown a positive investment potential.

----- CAMPGROUND MEMBERSHIP CONTRACTS -----

The Real Estate Agency also regulates the sale of campground memberships in Oregon. A **campground** is a camping site that does not have a permanent dwelling and is designed and promoted for the purposes of camping use by a trailer, tent, tent-trailer, recreational vehicle, pickup camper, etc. It is subject to regulation by the Agency when the campground is owned or operated by a membership camping contractor and is available for camping by purchasers of membership camping contracts. A membership camping contract grants a membership that provides a right or license to use the campgrounds and facilities of the membership camping operator for more than 30 days, (e.g., for a specific period, for the life of the member, or for an unlimited time with a right to transfer ownership by sale or will a limited or unlimited number of  times). Such a contract must be registered with the Agency before it can be offered or sold in Oregon. Agreements for nonmembership rental or use of state or county public campgrounds or private campgrounds such as KOA, are not considered membership camping contracts and do not have to be registered.

To register, the membership camping operator must provide certain information to the Agency, including:
- the operator's identity, experience in the camping club business, and ownership interest in the campground facilities.
- a description of the nature of the purchaser's license or right to use.
- a description of the facilities and services available to purchasers.
- any material encumbrances on the campground facilities.
- any reciprocal agreements that allow members to use other camping sites.
- a copy of the membership camping contract form.

After the Agency determines all required information has been filed, it will issue a certificate of registration, and memberships may be sold.

Persons selling these memberships must provide the same information provided the Agency to a purchaser in writing before the purchaser signs any contract or pays any money for the contract. A purchaser has a right of rescission within three business days, if the purchase is made at the campground, or within six business days, if it is made off site.

Campground memberships may be sold through membership camping contracts by the membership camping operator, membership camping contract salespersons registered with the operator, registered membership camping contract brokers, and real estate brokers and principal brokers. A membership camping operator and a membership camping contract salesperson registered with the operator may only engage in the initial sale of memberships. A registered membership camping contract broker may only engage in resales of memberships held by campground members.

A real estate broker or principal real estate broker is authorized to engage in the sale of campground memberships through membership camping contracts as long as the transaction is treated as any other real estate transaction, with the broker having a listing to sell memberships and complying with all rules and statutes relating to professional real estate activity. A broker may engage in initial sales of memberships listed with him by the campground operator or in resales of memberships listed by members.

A person cannot hold a real estate license and membership camping contract salesperson or broker registration at the same time.

Private Transactions by Licensees

----- PRIVATE TRANSACTIONS BY LICENSEES -----

While a person holds a real estate license, he is bound by and subject to the requirements of the law not only while engaging in professional real estate activity, but also while acting in his own behalf in a real estate transaction.

Transactions Subject to the Law

In order to prevent licensees from taking advantage of their superior knowledge of real estate in dealing with others, the license law requires that a real estate licensee comply with various statutory and Oregon Real Estate Agency administrative rules requirements in conducting professional real estate activity, whether for a client or directly or indirectly for himself, and whether his license is active or inactive.

A person with an active or inactive real estate license is subject to the requirements of the law while engaging in any professional real estate activity on behalf of others or while acting in his own behalf except for the lease or rental of a licensee's own real estate.

Therefore, sale of a licensee's own rental property would be subject to the normal license law requirements. Lease options of the licensee's own property would be subject to the same requirements, because they represent a negotiated purchase that may be consummated by the exercise of the option granted with the lease. However, the rental or lease of the licensee's own property is not subject to the requirements of the law.

A licensee, whether active or inactive, is subject to the requirements of the law and rules in any offer or transaction involving real property in which he has a named interest, whether as a tenant in severalty, tenant by the entirety, tenant in common or joint tenant.

> **For Example**
>
> Broker Bob owns a home with his wife as tenants by the entirety. The sale of that home is subject to all of the requirements for personal transactions, whether Bob handles the advertising and negotiations or his wife handles everything in the transaction.

The administrative rules do not allow a real estate licensee to use a business as a concealment of his ownership in order to avoid the requirements of the licensing law. They make a licensee subject to all of the requirements of the law in any offer or transaction entered into by a corporation, partnership, limited partnership or other legal entity, when the licensee is an owner of the entity and is at any time involved in the negotiations concerning the offer or transaction on behalf of that entity. A licensee is considered to be an owner in the legal entity and subject to the license law when he has an ownership interest equaling more than 5% of the total ownership interest. Therefore, if a licensee had a 10% interest in a limited partnership and was negotiating a sale or purchase of real property for the partnership, the licensee and the principal broker would be subject to the requirements of the real estate license law, even though the brokerage was not involved in the transaction at all.

<table>
<tr><td>For Example</td><td>Gary Henderson is an active principal broker and a major stockholder in Mid-Pacific Corporation. Mid-Pacific is offering to sell units in a condominium project the corporation owns. Henderson is actively participating in the negotiation for the sale of the units. To comply with the law, Henderson must treat the transaction as he would one for clients. This means, he will have to disclose his interest in the corporation, deposit any funds he receives in connection with the sale into a neutral escrow depository or clients' trust account, and maintain a file for the transaction as he would for any client's transaction.</td></tr>
</table>

If a licensee had stock in a corporation amounting to 10% ownership in the corporation, but was not engaged in any negotiations on behalf of the corporation, he would not be subject to the law. The only exception to this rule is a licensee who is the general partner in a qualified limited partnership. The law does not apply to a licensee acting as a general partner while engaging in the sale of limited partnership interests and while engaging in the acquisition, sale, exchange, lease, transfer or management of real estate of the limited partnership.

Requirements

The Real Estate Agency administrative rules require that any offer or negotiation for the sale, exchange, lease-option, or purchase of real estate on a licensee's own behalf by a principal broker or property manager must be handled as any other professional real estate activity of the licensee. This means any earnest money received must be deposited in a clients' trust account or escrow. Copies of signed documents must be given to the parties signing. Documents and records must be retained for six years. Most importantly, the licensee must adhere to the standards imposed on licensees in any transaction.

Any offer or transaction involving a sale, exchange, lease-option, or purchase of real estate by an active broker associated with a principal broker is subject to the supervision and control of the licensee's principal real estate broker. Therefore, a licensee involved in a personal transaction must inform his supervising broker of the transaction, provide copies of all documents in the transaction to the principal broker, have the principal broker review and initial all transaction documents, and have all funds placed in the principal broker's clients' trust account or into escrow. The principal broker must control the licensee's personal dealings in the same way as he does the licensee's other professional real estate activities, maintaining records for the transaction in the same manner as for transactions involving clients of the brokerage, and ensuring that the transaction conforms to all requirements of the real estate law.

Neither the law nor the rules require that an active real estate licensee list his property for sale with his principal broker or have his principal broker represent him as a buyer's representative in purchase transactions. After all, a licensee working at a commercial real estate brokerage should not be required to list a home with that company. A licensee working at a brokerage in Portland should not have to list his cottage in Bend with that company. A licensee should not be required to list property with anyone, since the purpose of the law is to protect the public. That is done by requiring supervision and holding the principal broker accountable for the actions of a licensee associated with him in that licensee's personal transactions.

A licensee may advertise his own property if the property is not listed for sale or lease with his principal broker, provided the ad identifies him as a licensee.

A licensee holding an inactive license may not engage in any professional real estate activity for others. However, when buying or selling on his own account, or when involved in the lease-option of personally owned real estate, he must:
- disclose the fact he has a real estate license on at least the first written offer or document of agreement.
- deposit all funds received in the transaction into a neutral escrow depository in Oregon, since he would not have a clients' trust account.
- adhere to the same recordkeeping requirements as if the transaction involved a client, i.e., maintain documents as if he were a principal broker handling the transaction.

Since he is inactive, his transactions are not supervised by a principal broker.

Disclosures

In addition to these requirements, the rules require that a licensee, whether active or inactive, disclose to the other party in the transaction that he is a real estate licensee. This disclosure of licensee status must be included in any advertising or display signs. While a broker associated with a principal broker who offers property for sale on his own behalf is required to disclose the fact that he has a real estate license, he is not required to state whether the license is active or inactive or to disclose the name of his principal broker in the ad or sign.

If the licensee lists the property through a principal broker, he need not make the disclosure in the ad or the sign, as the ad and sign will have the principal broker's name. The principal broker's sign and name will serve to make potential buyers aware that they will be dealing with a professional real estate agent. However, the principal broker would be required to maintain complete records of the lease-option transaction for six years, just as he would for any other professional real estate transaction handled for a client by a licensee associated with him.

The disclosure of license status must also appear on at least the first written agreement concerning the offer or transaction (e.g., the earnest money agreement, lease option, or exchange agreement). It must also state that the licensee is representing himself as either the buyer or the seller in the transaction.

Property Management

A licensed broker associated with a principal broker may engage in professional property management activity only in name of the principal broker. He may not manage property he has listed directly for an owner, set up a property management business outside of the broker's supervision, or be licensed to one principal broker for sales and at same time work under another principal broker or real estate property manager to perform property management. However, he may rent or lease personally owned rental properties outside the principal broker's supervision.

In addition, a property manager must comply with the license law and administrative rules in the lease-option of personally owned properties. Therefore, a property manager must disclose his license status if he is involved in the lease-option of his personally owned property and have funds received deposited in the clients' trust account or escrow. He would not have to comply with the law or rules into the rental of his personally owned properties. Therefore, he would not be required to place rental collections in a clients' trust account or an escrow account, maintain ledger accounts or make monthly accountings, maintain any records or advertising files for the rentals, and authorize inspections by the Real Estate Commissioner of any records he does maintain. He would do these things in his professional property management activity on behalf of clients.

Profit

A licensee may act on own behalf in a real estate transaction to make a profit. He may purchase property at a price below the market value. In fact, this is a specific provision in the statutes. Real estate licensees will buy and sell real estate for themselves in the course of their real estate careers. Sometimes a licensee will purchase property listed by his brokerage or other brokerages. Sometimes he will buy property offered for sale by owner. In either case, he may try to achieve a good deal. Often this will mean offering less than the seller's asking price and less than market value.

When a seller does not use the services of a broker, the licensee may negotiate the selling price down on the basis that the seller is saving the commission. When a seller does list the property, a licensee may negotiate a lower price on the basis of waiving his portion of the commission. Sometimes the licensee negotiates a favorable price because he is a skillful negotiator. In none of these instances would the seller have cause to complain that he was taken advantage of when selling for less than market value. The licensee is free to negotiate the best price possible, as long as he does not violate the law.

The same is true when a licensee sells a property. Just as with any seller he represents, a licensee is free to try to get the best price possible and is obligated to disclose all material facts to a potential buyer.

However, just as he would in any transaction in which he acted as an agent, he would have a duty to deal honestly and in good faith with a customer and disclose material facts known by him and not apparent or readily ascertainable to the customer. He must treat the buyer or seller with whom he is dealing, as he would a buyer or seller in a transaction in which he was acting as an agent, and document all pertinent communications to prevent any disputes and to defend against any claims that he may have demonstrated bad faith in the transaction.

State Fair Housing Law

Oregon law prohibits discrimination in selling, renting or leasing real property. Oregon's discrimination statutes related to real property transactions apply to everyone, including sellers and lessors of real property, as well as real estate licensees.

Prohibitions

The federal Fair Housing Act makes it unlawful to discriminate against people seeking to obtain housing. A wide range of housing related activities are covered by fair housing law, including renting, selling, lending, zoning and providing insurance. Under national fair housing laws, it is illegal to deny access to housing to people because of their race, color, national origin, religion, gender, familial status (the presence of children in a household) or disability. In Oregon, it is also illegal to discriminate in housing transactions based on a person's marital status, source of income (including, as of July 1, 2014, Housing Choice/Section 8 Vouchers), sexual orientation (including gender identity) or status as a domestic violence victim.

Therefore, a broker is not allowed to refuse to rent an apartment to someone because she is Iranian; a seller may not limit a sale to married couples or reject an offer to purchase because the purchaser is unmarried; a landlord may not rent only to tenants who belong to a minority race or restrict the rental to men only because the landlord expects the tenant to do repair work on the house; a landlord may not refuse to rent real property to someone on the basis that he was not born in the U.S., or he is an unmarried person.

No person can, because of the same characteristics, expel a purchaser from any real property. Therefore, a landlord cannot evict a tenant after the landlord discovers the tenant belongs to a religion the landlord does not like.

No person can, because of these characteristics, make any distinction, discrimination or restriction against a purchaser in the price, terms, conditions or privileges relating to the sale, rental, lease or occupancy of real property or in the furnishing of any facilities or services in connection with the property.

Therefore, sellers may not offer more favorable terms to purchasers who are of the same race as the seller. A landlord cannot legally reduce the rent of apartments for tenants who are married, but not for tenants who are single. A landlord could however require a prospective tenant to furnish credit references, require a tenant to pay a larger deposit because the tenant has a poor history of renting or even refuse to rent to a person who has a poor credit rating, since those actions are not based on race, religion, etc.

No person may discriminate by attempting to discourage the sale, rental or lease of any real property to a purchaser. Therefore a real estate licensee would violate the statute if he discouraged a prospective Hispanic purchaser from making an offer in a predominantly white neighborhood. A landlord would violate the law if he told a prospective minority tenant that an apartment was not available when, in fact, the apartment was vacant.

No person may publish, circulate, issue or display any communication, notice, advertisement or sign of any kind relating to the sale, rental or leasing of real property which indicates any preference, limitation, specification or discrimination based on race, color, national origin, religion, gender, familial status (the presence of children in a household) or disability. In Oregon, it is also illegal to discriminate in housing transactions based on a person's marital status, source of income (including, as of July 1, 2014, Housing Choice/Section 8 Vouchers), sexual orientation (including gender identity) or status as a domestic violence victim. Therefore, it would be illegal to advertise the rental of property to married couples only, to advertise a preference for black families, or to advertise a home for sale to mainstream Protestants only.

No person may assist, induce, incite or coerce another person to commit an act or engage in a practice that violates this law. Therefore, it is illegal to attempt to induce someone to refuse to rent an apartment to a person who belongs to a minority race.

It is illegal to coerce, intimidate, threaten or interfere with any person exercising or enjoying any right granted or protected by this law. It is also illegal to coerce, intimidate, threaten or interfere with a third party assisting another person in the exercise of his rights under this law.

In addition, no person may for profit influence any other person to sell or rent any dwelling by representations regarding the entry or possible entry into the neighborhood of a person belonging to a protected class.

In the sale, lease or rental of real estate, no person may disclose to any person that an occupant or owner of real property has or died from human immunodeficiency virus (HIV) or acquired immune deficiency syndrome (AIDS).

No real estate licensee may accept or retain a listing of real property for sale, lease or rental with an understanding that a purchaser may be discriminated against with respect to the sale, rental or lease because of race, color, sex, marital status, familial status, religion, national origin, physical or mental handicap. Therefore, a real estate broker cannot accept a listing with the understanding that the owner will only sell to an unmarried man or that the property will not be shown to those with mental handicaps. He cannot accept a listing if the seller requires the broker to show the property only to purchasers who are Caucasians or if the seller tells the broker he will not accept offers from purchasers who are Hispanics.

Once he has a listing, a real estate licensee might be found guilty of violating Oregon's discrimination statutes if he retains the listing with the knowledge that the owner refuses to sell to anyone who belongs to a different religion than the owner.

Since based on marital status is covered by Oregon statute, a broker cannot retain a listing if a few days after an owner signed the listing agreement he told the broker that he would not sell to anyone who was single or divorced.

 No person or other entity whose business includes engaging in residential real estate-related transactions may discriminate against any person's participation in a transaction or in the terms or conditions of the transaction because of race, color, national origin, religion, gender, familial status (the presence of children in a household) or disability. In Oregon, it is also illegal to discriminate in housing transactions based on a person's marital status, source of income (including, as of July 1, 2014, Housing Choice/Section 8 Vouchers), sexual orientation (including gender identity) or status as a domestic violence victim.

Residential real estate related-transaction includes making or purchasing loans or providing other financial assistance for purchasing, constructing, improving repairs in or maintaining a dwelling; or for securing residential real estate. It also includes selling, brokering or appraising residential real property.

Familial status under the law means the relationship between one or more individuals who have not attained 18 years of age and who are domiciled with:

- a parent or another person having legal custody of the individual; or
- the designee of the parent or other person having custody, with the written permission of the parent or other person.

The term also includes any individual, regardless of age or domicile, who is pregnant or is in the process of securing legal custody of an individual who has not attained 18 years of age.

Purchaser includes an occupant, prospective occupant, lessee, prospective lessee, buyer or prospective buyer.

Exclusions

Unlike federal law, which has a number of exclusions, the state fair housing law has only three.

The law does not apply with respect to sex distinction, discrimination or restriction if the real property involved is such that the application of the law would necessarily result in common use of bath or bedroom facilities by unrelated person of the opposite sex. Therefore, a real estate broker in Oregon is allowed by law to refuse to rent a home to unrelated persons of the opposite sex who would share the same bathroom.

In addition, the law does not prohibit actions based on familial status or sex with regard to renting of space in a single-family home actually occupied as the owner's primary residence, if all occupants would share some common space within the residence.

The law does not apply to familial status distinction, discrimination or restriction with respect to housing for older persons. As used in this law, "housing for older persons" means housing:

- provided under any state or federal program specifically designed and operated to assist elderly persons, as defined by the state or federal program;
- intended for, and solely occupied by, persons 62 years of age or older; or
- intended and operated for occupancy by at least one person 55 years of age or older per unit. This housing qualifies as housing for older persons if at least 80% of the dwellings are occupied by at least one person per unit who is 55 years of age or older and the demonstrated and adhered-to intent of the owner or manager, as set forth in the policies and procedures for the housing, indicate that the housing is provided for persons 55 years of age or older.

Complaints and Enforcement

A person with a grievance may, by himself or with an attorney, make, sign, or file with Commissioner of the **Bureau of Labor and Industries**, a verified complaint in writing which states the name and address of the person or place of accommodation alleged to have committed the violation and sets forth the particulars and any other information the Labor Commissioner deems pertinent.

For Example	Connie Green, a resident of Eugene, believes she has been kept from buying a piece of real property because of her marital status. If Ms. Green wants to report her allegations and request an investigation, she should send her report to the Commissioner of the Bureau of Labor for the State of Oregon.

In addition, the Attorney General or the Commissioner of Labor may file a complaint whenever he has reason to believe a violation occurred.

After a complaint is filed, the Labor Commissioner may pursue an investigation of the complaint, during which additional persons may be added a respondents. If the facts warrant, the Labor Commissioner may take immediate steps through conference, conciliation, and persuasion to effect a settlement of the complaint. The terms of any settlement will then be contained in written conciliation agreement filed with Labor Commissioner. The terms may be relaxed if they would cause undue hardship to the respondent or others and are not essential to the protection of the complainant's rights.

If a settlement cannot be reached, the Labor Commissioner may hold a hearing, after which he may dismiss the charge or issue a cease-and-desist order. He may also fine a person up to $1,000 per violation.

> **NOTE:** A real estate licensee who has been found guilty of violating Oregon's discrimination statutes may face not only civil penalties imposed on him by the Labor Commissioner, but also disciplinary action taken against his real estate license by the Real Estate Commissioner. However, the Real Estate Commissioner could not impose a monetary fine against him for such a violation.

Any conciliation agreement and cease-and-desist order may be enforced by court order, a writ of mandamus to enforce the order or agreement, or a suit for specific performance of the order.

Brain Teaser

Reinforce your understanding of the material by correctly completing the following sentences:

1. When writing an offer to purchase, a licensee must include all of the _____ and _____ of the real estate transaction in the offer.

2. Bid _____, who merely spot bidders, do not need to be licensed.

3. A licensee is considered to be an owner in the legal entity and subject to the license law when he has an ownership interest equaling more than ___% of the total ownership interest.

4. Oregon's fair housing law provides that no person may, on account of race, color, sex, _____ status, familial status, religion, national origin, physical or mental handicap of any person, or source of _____ refuse to sell, lease or rent any real property to a purchaser.

Brain Teaser Answers

1. When writing an offer to purchase, a licensee must include all of the **terms** and **conditions** of the real estate transaction in the offer.

2. Bid **assistants**, who merely spot bidders, do not need to be licensed.

3. A licensee is considered to be an owner in the legal entity and subject to the license law when he has an ownership interest equaling more than **5**% of the total ownership interest.

4. Oregon's fair housing law provides that no person may, on account of race, color, sex, **marital** status, familial status, religion, national origin, physical or mental handicap of any person, or source of **income** refuse to sell, lease or rent any real property to a purchaser.

Review — Oregon Sales

This lesson covers requirements relating to buying and selling real estate.

Offers

An offer to purchase need not be written on any particular form approved or reviewed by the Agency. It must include all of the terms and conditions of the transaction, including whether the transaction is to be accomplished by way of deed or land sales contract, whether and at what time evidence of title is to be furnished to the prospective purchaser, and the type of earnest money received. A licensee must give the individual signing a true and legible copy and promptly tender the offer to the offeree or to his agent. He cannot hold offers pending the seller's decision on any previous offers or reject an offer without consulting the principal. He must ensure that each party receives a completed copy of the agreement within a reasonable time after both parties have signed it.

Auctions, Timeshares, Camping Contracts

An auctioneer and any bid assistants, who will answer questions about the real estate while a real estate auction is in progress, must be licensed, and the auction must comply with all real estate license law and Agency regulations.

Persons selling timeshares are subject to the real estate licensing laws and administrative rules. However, timeshare programs of 12 or fewer interests and timeshare programs for the shared use of personal property (e.g., motor homes, boats, airplanes) are not subject to timesharing and real estate licensing laws, although they are subject to other consumer protection laws, such as the property condition disclosure law. Timeshare purchasers must be given a public report and a five-calendar-day right of rescission.

Individuals or real estate marketers who are engaged in direct contacts with Oregon prospects by phone or in person to solicit their presence for a sales presentation must be licensed. The marketing may be done by real estate licensees or through a separately licensed real estate marketing organization (REMO). The REMO is licensed and supervised by one or more principal persons who are screened by the Agency and operates through employees registered with the Agency. A broker should not promote the availability of an exchange program as the main selling point of a sales presentation for a timeshare plan or promote a vacation timeshare for its investment potential.

A membership camping contract must be registered with the Agency before it can be offered or sold in Oregon. A membership camping operator and a membership camping contract salesperson registered with the membership camping operator may only engage in the initial sale of memberships. A registered membership camping contract broker may engage only in resales of memberships held by campground members. A real estate broker or principal broker may engage in initial sales of memberships listed with him by the campground operator or in resales of memberships listed by members. A person cannot hold a real estate license and membership camping contract salesperson or broker registration at the same time.

Private Transactions by Licensees

A person with any real estate license is subject to the requirements of the law while acting in his own behalf in the offer to, negotiations for, or the actual sale, exchange, lease-option, or purchase of real estate, but not in the lease or rental of his own real estate. He is subject to all of the requirements of the law in any offer or transaction entered into by a corporation, partnership, limited partnership or other legal entity, when he is at least a 5% owner of the entity and is at any time an active participant in or participates in the negotiations concerning the offer or transaction on behalf of that entity.

Any offer or negotiation for the sale, exchange, lease-option, or purchase of real estate on a licensee's own behalf must be handled as any other professional real estate activity, with earnest money deposited in a clients' trust account or escrow, and copies of signed documents given to the parties signing, to the principal broker for review and to be retained for six years. A licensee may advertise his own property if the property is not listed for sale or lease with his principal broker, provided the ad identifies him as a licensee.

A licensee holding an inactive license must deposit funds received into a neutral escrow depository in Oregon and adhere to recordkeeping requirements as if the transaction involved a client.

In addition, a licensee, whether active or inactive, must disclose to the other party that he is a real estate licensee on at least the first written document of agreement concerning the offer or transaction and, unless he lists his property with a principal broker, in any advertising or display signs.

State Fair Housing Law

Oregon law provides that no person may, because of race, color, national origin, religion, gender, familial status (the presence of children in a household), disability, marital status, source of income (including, as of July 1, 2014, Housing Choice/Section 8 Vouchers), sexual orientation (including gender identity) or status as a domestic violence victim, refuse to sell, lease or rent any real property to a person of a protected class. The law does not apply to the following:

- With respect to sex distinction, discrimination or restriction if application of the law would necessarily result in the common use of bath or bedroom facilities by unrelated persons of the opposite sex
- Actions based on familial status or sex with regard to renting of space in the owner's single-family primary residence, if all occupants would share some common space within the residence
- Familial status distinction, discrimination or restriction with respect to housing for older persons

A person may file a written complaint with Commissioner of the Bureau of Labor.